BRAIN

kids

WORD SCRAMBLE!

Publications International, Ltd.

Cover Puzzle: Stephen Ryder

Puzzle Constructors: Cihan Altay, Myles Callum, Don Cook, Harvey Estes, David Millar, Michael Moreci, Alan Olschwang, Stephen Ryder, Pete Sarjeant, Fraser Simpson, Wayne Robert Williams

Illustrators: Erin Burke, Jen Torche

Contributing Writer: Holli Fort

Louis Weber, CEO
Publications International, Ltd.
7373 North Cicero Avenue
Lincolnwood, Illinois 60712

ISBN-13: 978-1-4508-2346-3
ISBN-10: 1-4508-2346-7

Manufactured in China.

8 7 6 5 4 3 2 1

LET THE GECKOS BE YOUR GUIDES

Welcome to *Brain Games™ Kids: Word Scramble!* You'll find tons of different word puzzles, including One Up, Crunched Letters, Tile Tie-Ins, and so much more.

Your guides on this puzzling journey will be three gecko friends: Gene, Gina, and Gus. You'll encounter these reptiles throughout the book, and wherever they appear, you'll find a tip or trick to help you along, or a fun fact to add to your knowledge of language—and, of course, geckos. You'll also want to keep an eye peeled for the Gecko-pedia, where you'll find tantalizing tidbits about puzzles and language.

Gene

Speaking of language, there's one important thing to note about these puzzles: We're not trying to trip you up, so all of the words used in the puzzles are ones that you can find in any dictionary. Maybe keep one close by in order to keep transforming those tiles into words. Leafing through a dictionary can really get your language juices going, so don't be apprehensive to thumb through its pages from time to time.

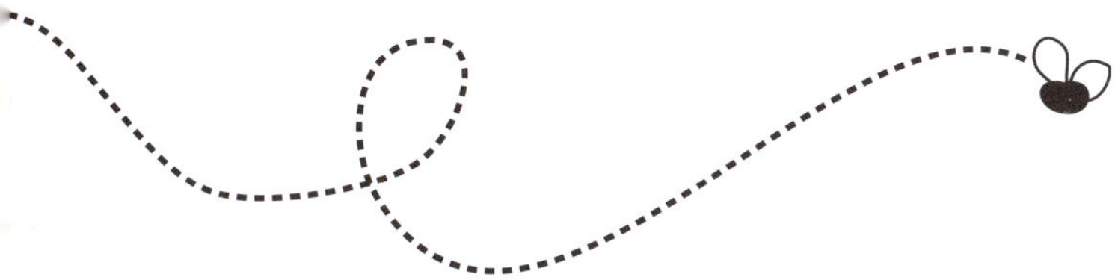

If you want to get a "geckologically sound" base for jumping into these puzzles, try following these handy tips:

Gina

Get the Lay of the Land

First things first: Make sure you read the directions, so you know what you're getting into and can avoid sticky situations. For example, for some of these puzzles, it doesn't matter what order you solve the clues in, but for others, you have to start in a particular place (say, at the bottom) and build on the clues to work your way to the end. Other puzzles may have word pairs that are similar or opposite—you'll never know unless you pay attention to the directions!

The Fly's the Limit

You'll notice that every puzzle has a fly icon. The number of flies—one, two, or three—tells you how hard a puzzle will be. You may want to start with a one-fly puzzle then work your way up to completing the three-fly puzzles. But remember, different kids find different puzzles buzz worthy, so you may find that a certain kind of three-fly puzzle is a snap, but there might be a one-fly puzzle that you swat at for days.

Change the Pattern

If you get stuck, try thinking of the puzzle in a different way. For puzzles with jumbled letters, try writing down the letters in a random pattern on the page, instead of in a straight line. That may help you visualize possible connections in a different way. Even a simple change in the way you're looking at the puzzle can make the solution become clearer.

Gus

Sticky Situations

If you get stuck on a puzzle, there are some simple things you can do to help get unstuck. If the puzzle is one where answers build on each other, step back and make sure that your answers to all the previous clues are correct. One wrong step along the way can cause big problems later. If the puzzle is one that doesn't have to be solved in order, go ahead and fill in the easiest answers first, and use them to help you figure out the harder answers. And if all else fails, take a break and come back to it later. Switch to a different puzzle for a little while, and when you come back, you may have a new perspective.

The puzzles in *Brain Games™ Kids: Word Scramble!* are designed to keep you on your (very sticky) toes, but just as important, to make sure you have fun in the process. So slither on in, pick your puzzle, and get started!

ONE UP

Use the 3 tiles at the bottom of the page to solve the bottom clue. Once you do that, move up the page, solving each clue as you go. Carry all the letters used from one clue to the next, rearranging them in the empty spaces.

Word	Clue
_ _ _ E _ _ _ _ _	Narrow party decorations
_ _ _ _ _ S _ _	Sides of some chairs
_ _ _ R _ _ _	More intelligent
_ _ _ _ _ R	Servant's employer
_ _ _ A _	Water vapor
S _ _ _	Plant stalk
_ _ _	Encountered

E T M

Answer on page 171.

ADD-A-LETTER

Rearrange the tiles from each word, adding one new tile from the bottom in order to form the name of a zoo animal in the empty boxes. Each tile from the bottom of the page is used only once.

O I L | ☐☐☐☐

G R I T | ☐☐☐☐☐

R E B | ☐☐☐☐

M A L L | ☐☐☐☐☐

M A L E | ☐☐☐☐☐

S N O B | ☐☐☐☐☐

C A N I A E

I know this "E" fits in the puzzle, but I don't know where. I bet you can figure it out!

Answer on page 171.

REWORD REWIND

Unscramble the tiles to form words that will complete the sentence.

A R E P S

Cavemen may have used a _ _ _ _ _

to get juicy green _ _ _ _ _ off of a tree.

Level

CHAIN WORDS

Place 3 letters in the middle squares that will complete one word and start another. For example, TAR would complete GUI – TAR – GET.

V	A	C				H	E	M

Answers on page 171.

ALPHABET EXPRESS

Use every letter tile below to complete the grid with common words.

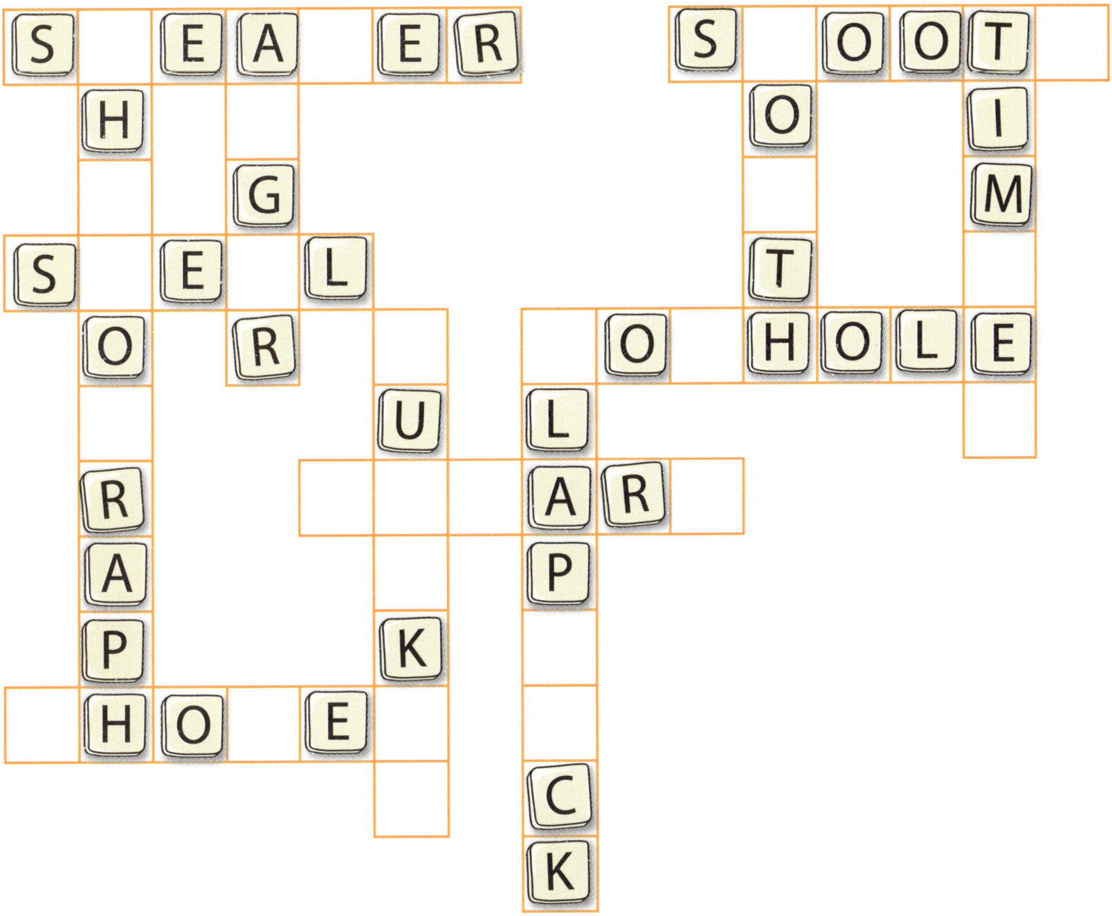

A B C D E F G H I

J K L M N O P Q

R S T U V W X Y Z

Answer on page 171.

WORD SWATTER

Use 3 letters from the word below to create 8 common words. Letters will be used more than once but will not repeat in each word.

K I N D L E

		E				K	
	D						D
K					I		
		N		D			

Did you know that geckos have special pads on our feet that help us climb walls? We do!

Gecko-pedia

The most commonly used word in the English language is "the." You have to get all the way to number 50 before you find "me"!

Answer on page 171.

TILE TIE-INS

Using the letter tiles below, complete the grid to reveal 9 characters from "Harry Potter."

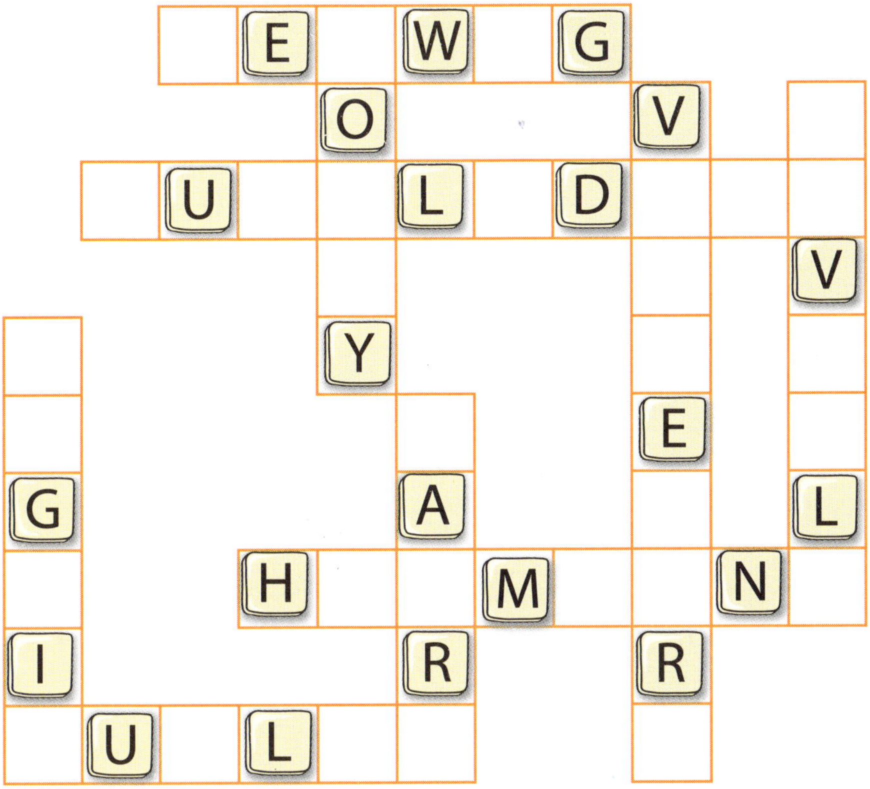

Answer on page 171.

DROP LETTERS

Use all 3 letter tiles to create 4-letter words below.
Each tile will be used once per word.

B S U

		G	
			Y
			H
C			
	N		
	T		

Answer on page 171.

LETTER GRIDLOCK

Use the given tiles to complete the grid with words reading across and down. Use the clues, which are assorted randomly, to help discover the missing words.

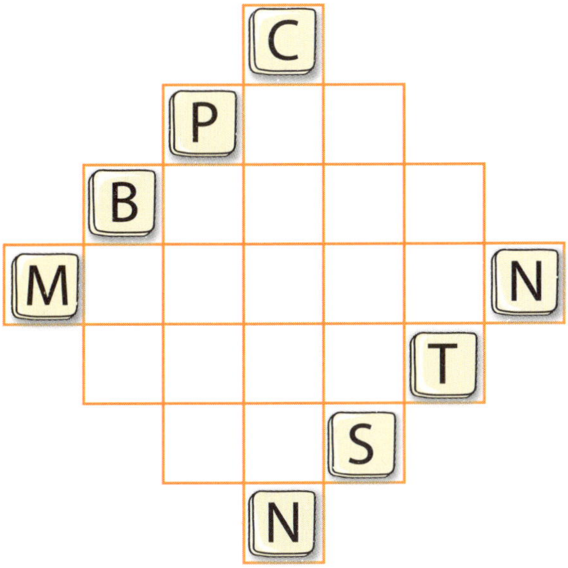

CLUES

- Uncovers
- Took a seat
- Straps to a horse's bridle
- Sack
- Really big guy
- Miles ___ hour
- France's capital
- Auntie, to mom
- Alien from the fourth planet
- Absolutely sure

Answer on page 172.

COME TOGETHER

Place each of the tile sets into the empty spaces below to create 3 nine-letter countries. Each tile set is used only once.

GUA GAP EZU

VEN ARA ORE

SIN NIC ELA

Answer on page 172.

THEME PARK

This "ride" has a theme, but we can't tell you what it is. Place all the words in the boxes below—when you do, read the word created in the outlined boxes, from top to bottom, to reveal what the theme is.

CANDY
COSTUME
GHOSTS
GOBLINS
MAKEUP
MASK
ZOMBIES

Answer on page 172.

CRUNCHED LETTERS

Create 3 words by placing the letter tiles into the grid. Two tiles will be added to the 3-letter sets given—one letter at the beginning and another at the end.

	O	M	E	
	O	M	E	
	O	M	E	

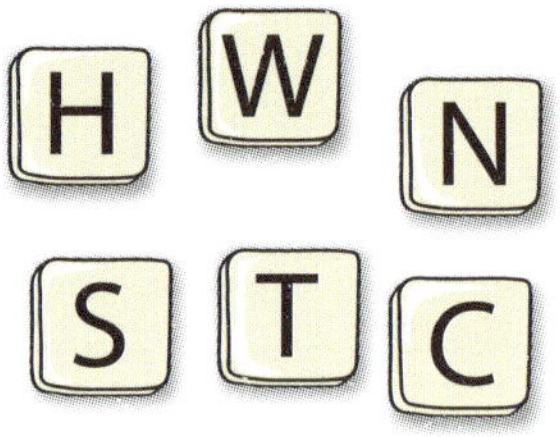

Gecko-pedia

At 15 letters, "uncopyrightable" is the longest English isogram, a word or phrase that doesn't repeat a letter. Some fun isogram phrases include "jack-in-the-box," "magic flute," "flying saucer," and "king of hearts."

Answer on page 172

CROSSED OUT

Use the given tiles to spell a pair of related words that meet on the given letter.

A T P S I

R U G M U

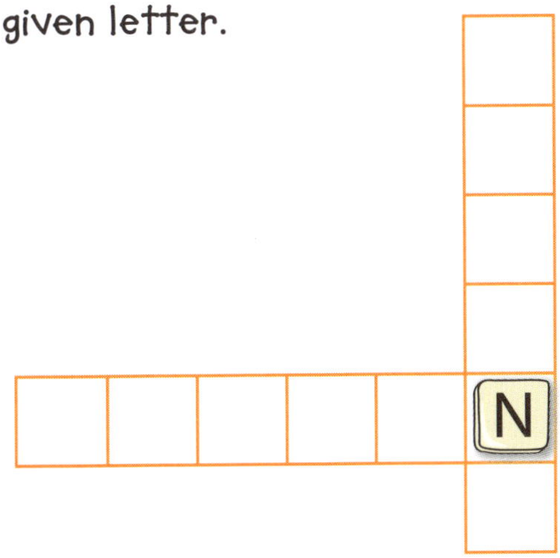

evel

SHUFFLE BOARD

Rearrange each of the letters in the tile groups below to form words. Place the new words into the grid. One letter has already been placed.

E M I T S

Q U A D S

Q U I T E

R I M E S

S T R A D

Answers on page 172.

WORD SWATTER

Use 4 letters from the word below to create 8 common words. Letters will be used more than once but will not repeat in each word.

T E A S P O O N

	P			
		O		
	N			
	T			

N				
		P		
				T
	T			

Answer on page 172

FITTING TILES

In this miniature crossword, the clues are listed randomly. It is up to you to figure out the placement of the 9 answers. To help you, we've inserted 2 letters in the grid, and this is the only occurrence of those letters in the completed puzzle.

CLUES

- Japanese cartoons
- Opposite of first
- Quizzes in school
- Tag on a T-shirt
- Put in chips at the start of a poker game
- Send out
- Spill mark
- Part of a microscope or telescope
- Prejudice

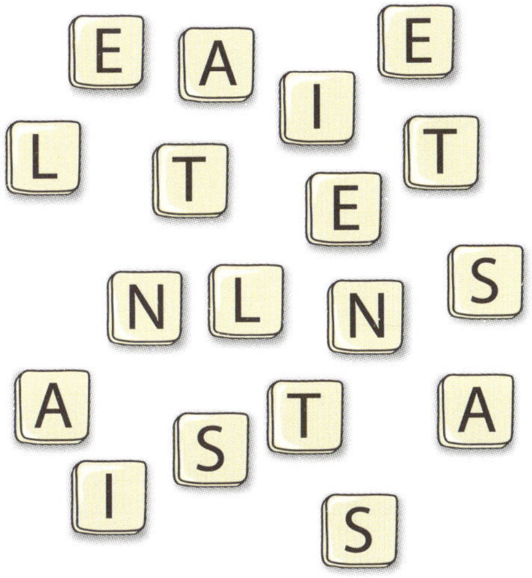

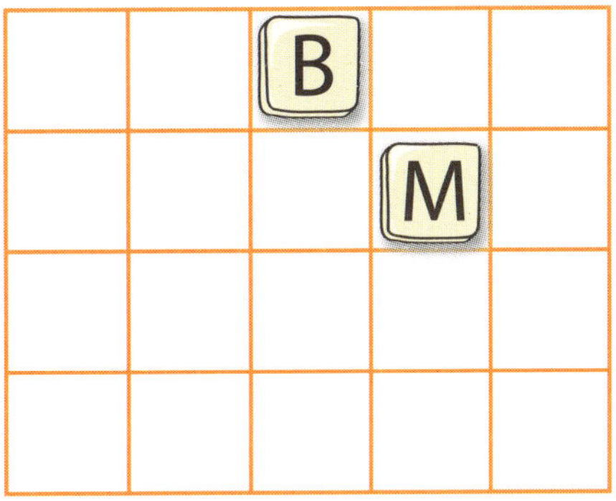

Answer on page 172.

DROP LETTERS

Use all 3 letter tiles to create 4-letter words below.
Each tile will be used once per word.

I R T

S			
			P
D			
		O	
G			
			M

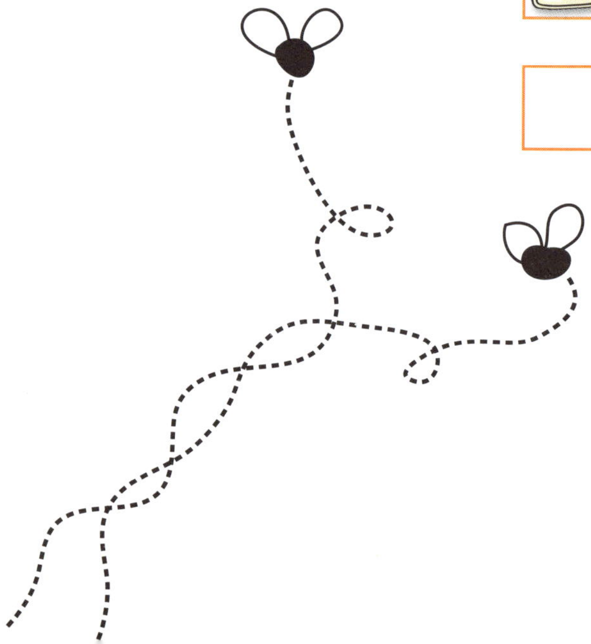

Answer on page 172

REPEAT REPEAT

Use the 8 tiles given to complete each pair of words.
Each pair will use the same 4 letter tiles in the same order.

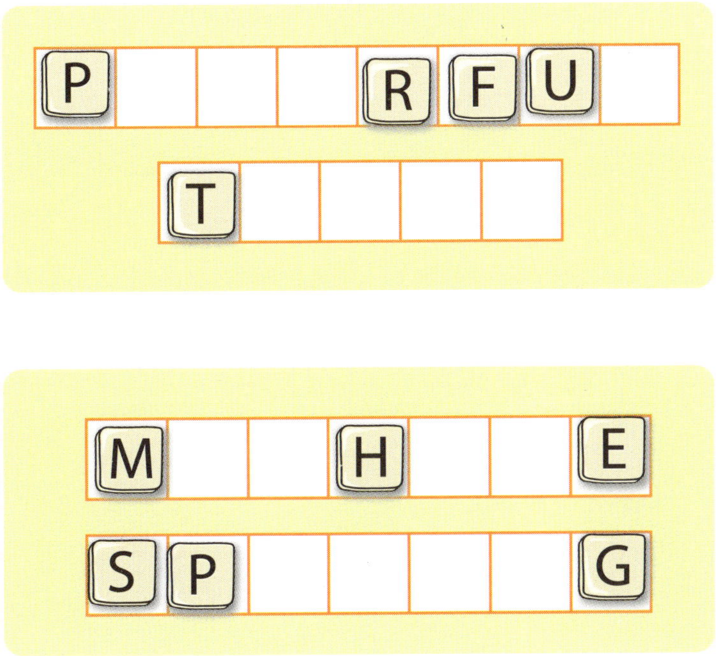

Answer on page 172.

WORD STICKERS

Use the letter tiles given to complete the word pairs.
Each pair of words will be an antonym (opposite) of one another.

E K A
H B I L

			C	
W			T	

R A
F A E

N			

		R

Answer on page 173

ONE UP

Use the 3 tiles at the bottom of the page to solve the bottom clue. Once you do that, move up the page, solving each clue as you go. Carry all the letters used from one clue to the next, rearranging them in the empty spaces.

_ _ U _ _ _ _ _ _ ..... Traveler's mementos

V _ _ _ _ _ _ _ ..... Particular variations

_ _ _ I _ _ _ ..... Elders

_ _ _ S _ _ ..... Detection device

_ _ _ R _ ..... Sleep noisily

_ _ _ E ..... Sense organ

_ _ _ ..... Dad's boy

O S N

Answer on page 173.

ALPHABET EXPRESS

Use every letter tile below to complete the grid with common words.

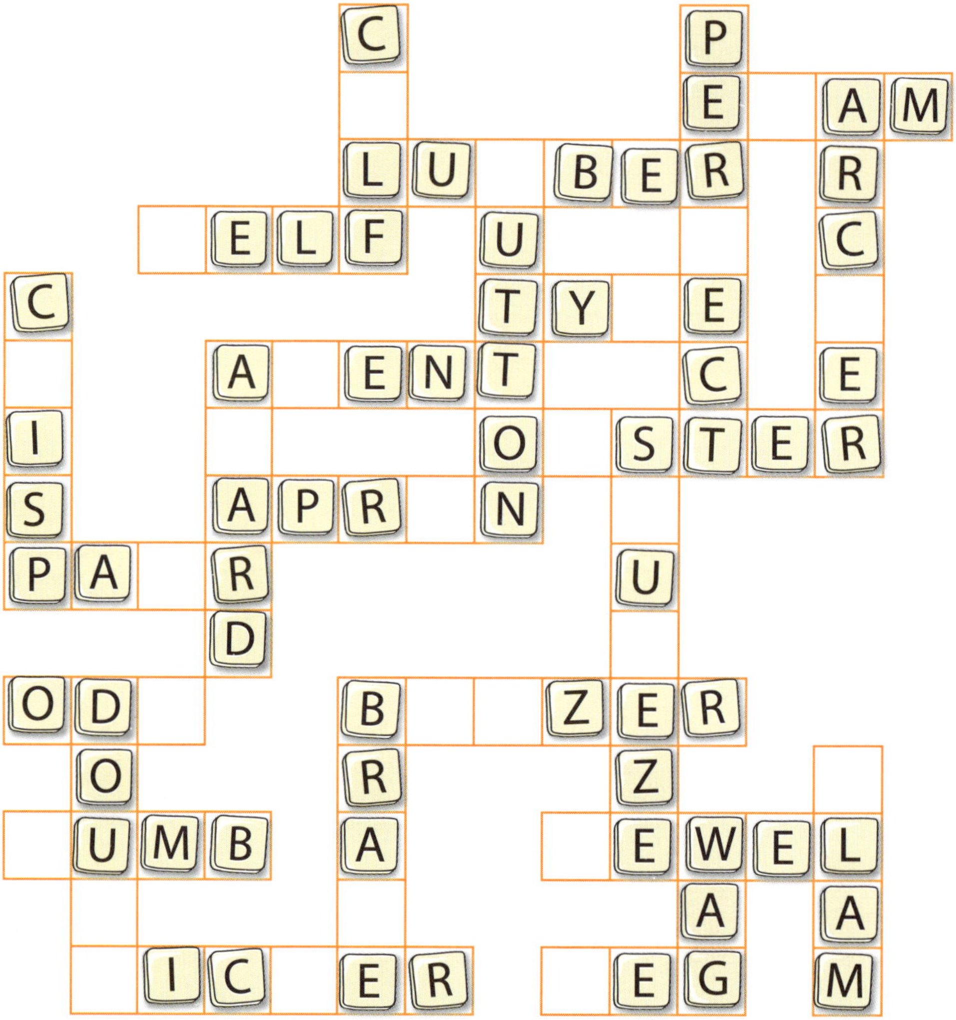

A B C D E F G H I

J K L M N O P Q

R S T U V W X Y Z

Answer on page 173.

LETTER GRIDLOCK

Use the given tiles to complete the grid with words reading across and down. Use the clues, which are assorted randomly, to help discover the missing words.

CLUES

- Animal that seems to wear a mask
- Ballerinas, for example
- Bedtime tale
- Emergency signal
- Like a desert
- Looks closely
- Makes a big fuss
- Partners of Mas
- Walked back and forth
- Eminem's music

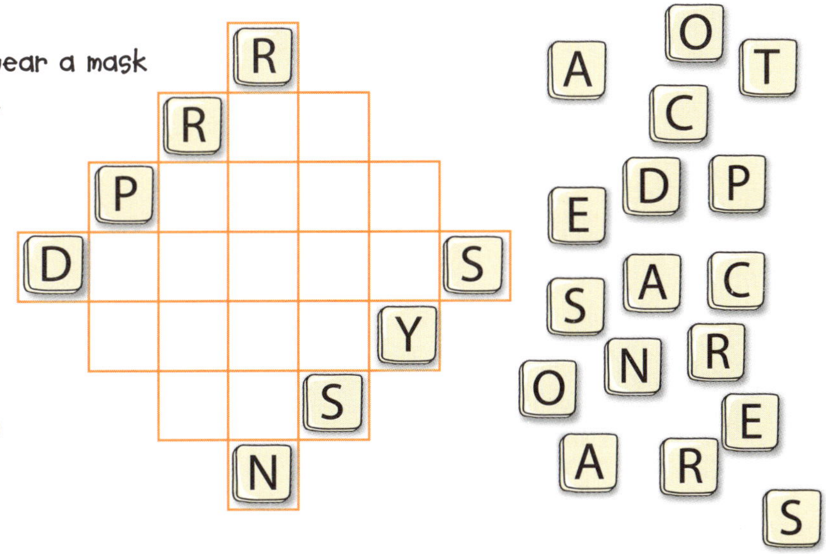

evel

JUMBLED UP

Place each letter into the empty boxes below to create a common word. Tiles are in the correct order, but they are not in the upright position.

Answers on page 173.

TILE TIE-INS

Using the letter tiles below, complete the grid to reveal the names of Santa's 9 reindeer.

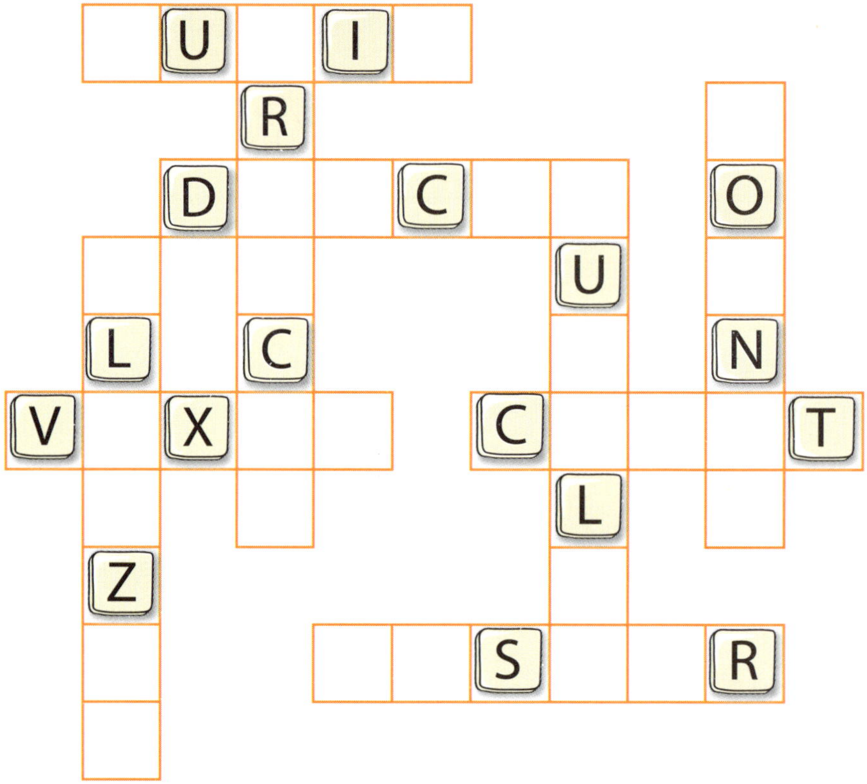

Answer on page 173

PILES O' TILES

Place all the tiles into the grid so they spell Canadian-themed words. The tiles are compiled in specific groups—those groups will appear together in across or down entries.

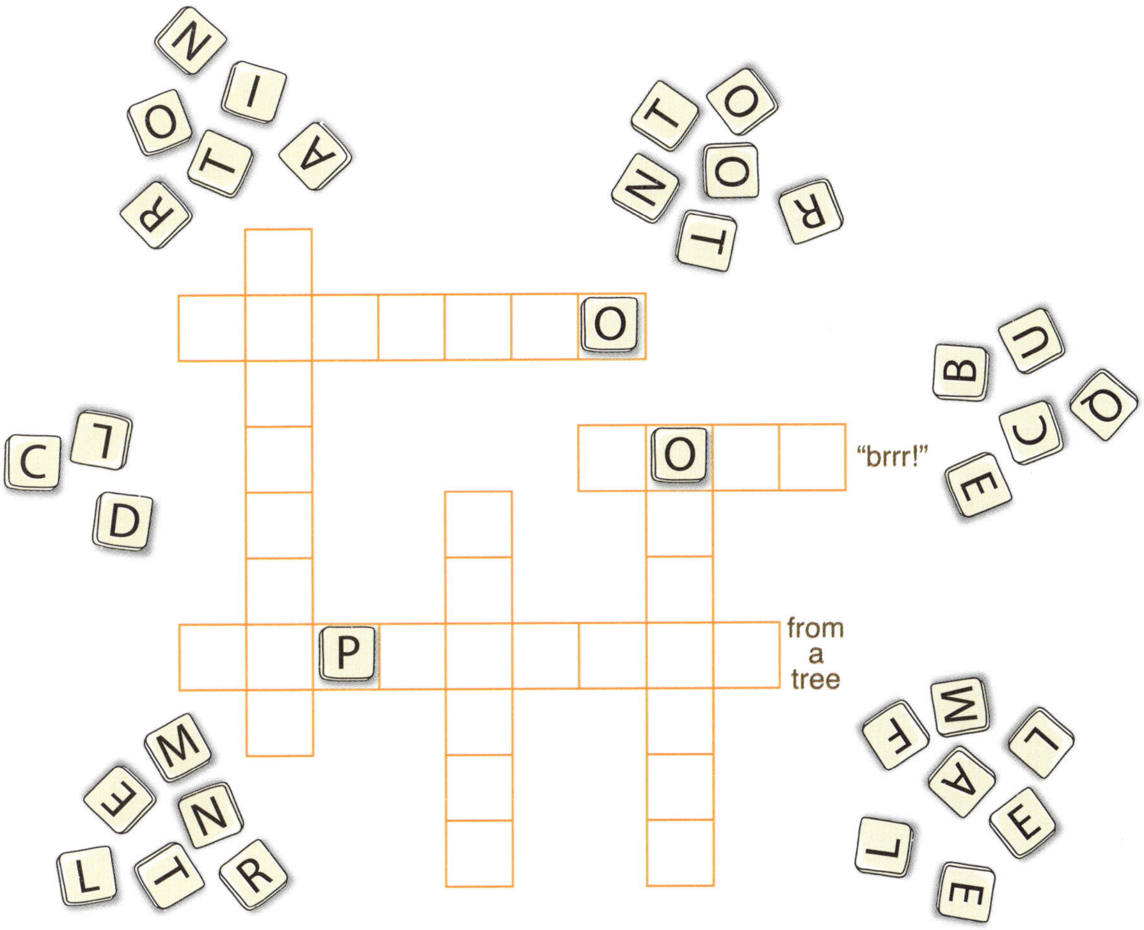

Answer on page 173.

ADD-A-LETTER

Rearrange the tiles from each word, adding one new tile from the bottom in order to form a word related to golf in the empty boxes. Each tile from the bottom of the page is used only once.

R I D E ☐☐☐☐☐

R I O ☐☐☐☐

P I C ☐☐☐☐

B R I D E ☐☐☐☐☐☐

G A L E ☐☐☐☐☐

T A R ☐☐☐☐

I S L E ☐☐☐☐☐

C E N I P V H

Answer on page 174

PLUS ONE

Using the letters in the top 3 tiles, create 3 new 4-letter words by adding one of the letters from the bottom 3 tiles.

L A P

M E F

A I D

C E P

Answer on page 174.

WORD SWATTER

Use 3 letters from the words below to create 5 common words. Letters will be used more than once but will not repeat in each word.

S A T U P

P			
		T	
	U		
T			
	P		

Answer on page 174

SHUFFLE BOARD

Rearrange each of the letters in the words below to form new words. Place the new words into the grid. One letter has already been placed.

L A M P   N A P

P O E M S   S A P

P O T   S P O O N

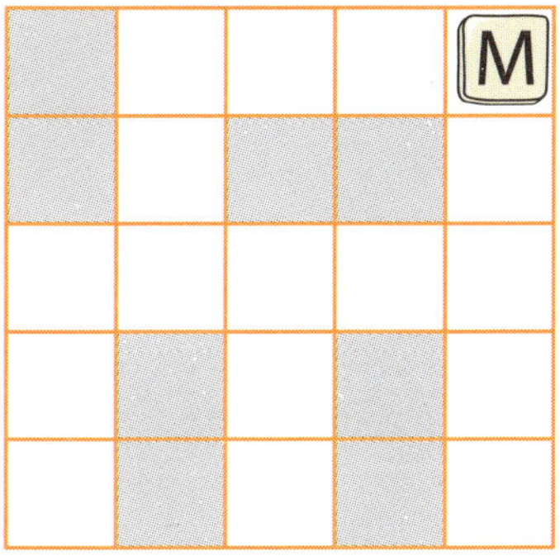

REWORD REWIND

Unscramble the tiles to form words that will complete the sentence.

A T R S

The _ _ _ _ were neat,

but the lion was the _ _ _ _ of the zoo.

Answers on page 174.

CRUNCHED LETTERS

Create 3 words by placing the letter tiles into the grid. Two tiles will be added to the 3-letter sets given—one letter at the beginning and another at the end.

	L	A	M	
	L	A	M	
	L	A	M	

Answer on page 174

COME TOGETHER

Place each of the tile sets into the empty spaces below to create 3 nine-letter foods. Each tile set is used only once.

A S P	S P A	T T I
S E R	A R A	G H E
G U S	O L E	C A S

Answer on page 174.

FITTING TILES

In this miniature crossword, the clues are listed randomly. It is up to you to figure out the placement of the 9 answers. To help you, we've inserted 2 letters in the grid, and this is the only occurrence of those letters in the completed puzzle.

CLUES

- Very stubborn animal
- Zodiac sign showing a set of scales
- Not imaginary
- Opposite of minor
- Pokes with a pencil
- Three-legged stand used by artists
- Largest continent
- Mean character in a fairy tale
- Cell phone minutes tally

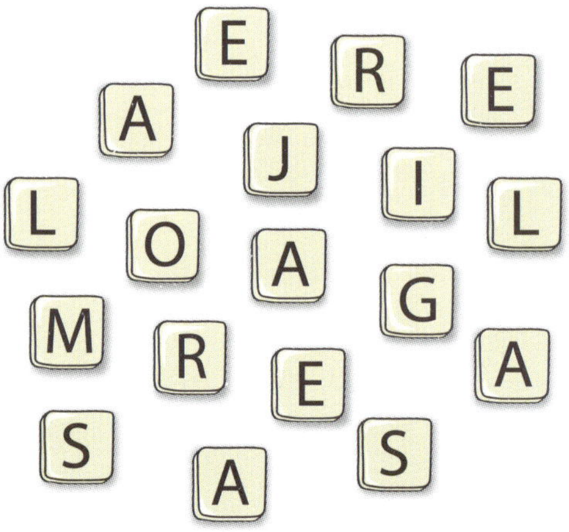

U				
		B		

Answer on page 174

WORD STICKERS

Use the letter tiles given to complete the word pairs. Each pair of words will be a homonym (words that sound alike, but are spelled differently) of one another.

R U E R
F L L O

F			W		

		O		

S A R T
T E S R

		A		

			I	

Answer on page 174.

THEME PARK

This "ride" has a theme, but we can't tell you what it is. Place all the words in the boxes below—when you do, read the word created in the outlined boxes, from top to bottom, to reveal what the theme is.

CLAM	PORPOISE	SWORDFISH
GROUPER	SHARK	TUNA
JELLYFISH	SQUID	WHALE
OCTOPUS	STING RAY	

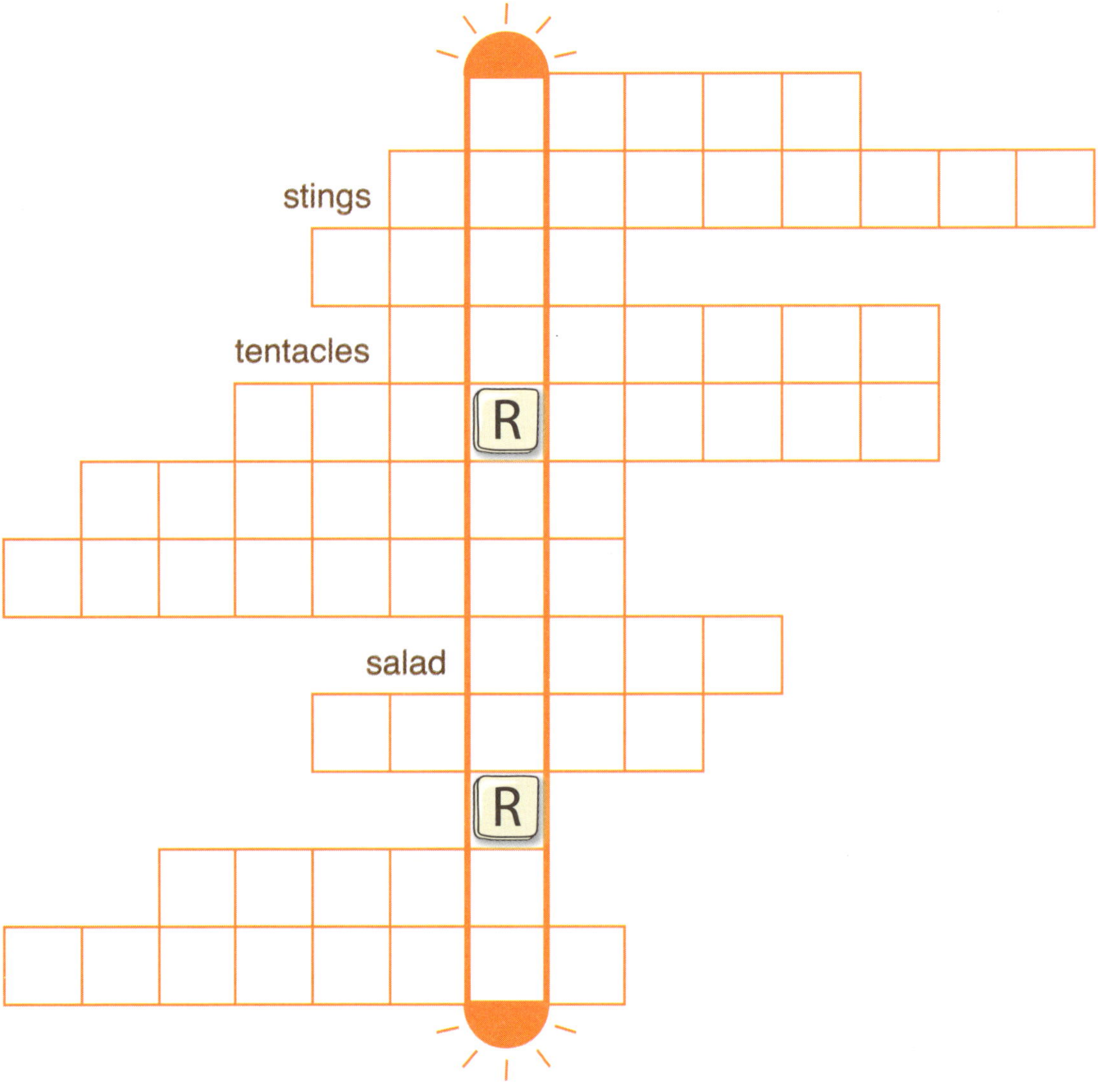

Answer on page 174

SHUFFLE BOARD

Rearrange each of the letters in the words below to form new words. Place the new words into the grid. One letter has already been placed.

M A T E S   P A S S

M O A T S   P O R T S

W R O T E

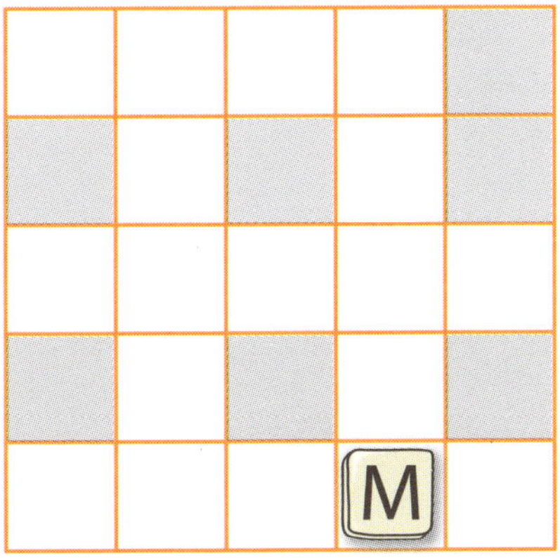

evel

CROSSED OUT

Use the given tiles to spell a pair of related words that meet on the given letter.

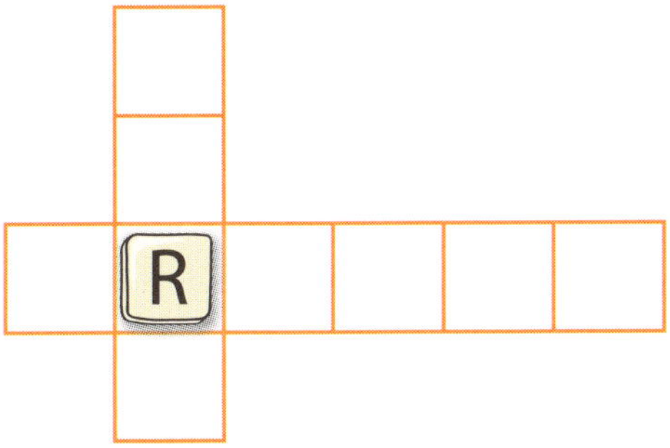

H T B K

A G D I

Answers on page 175.

ALPHABET EXPRESS

Use every letter tile below to complete the grid with common words.

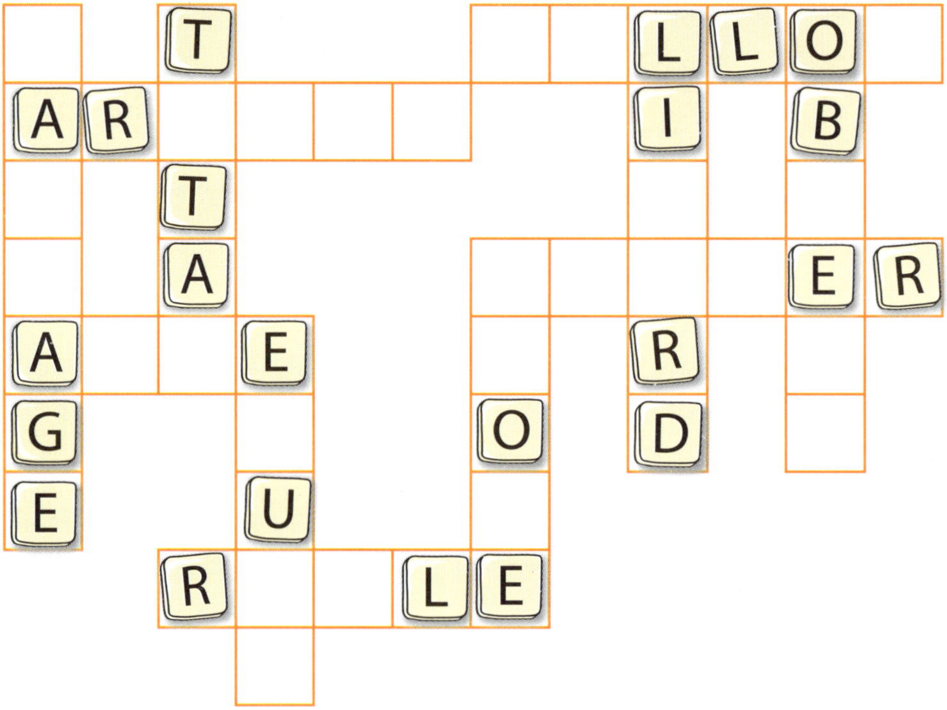

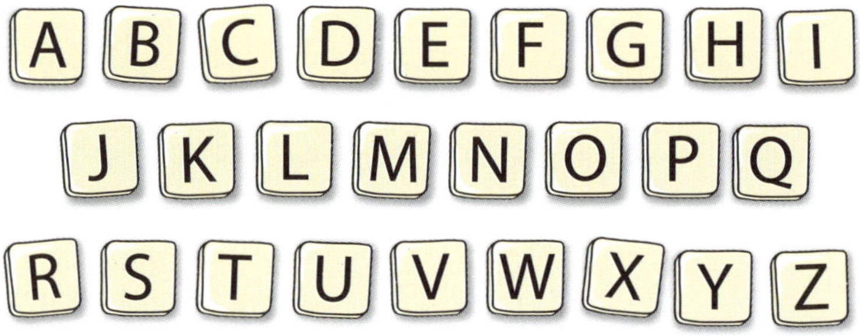

Answer on page 175

PILES O' TILES

Place all the tiles into the grid so they spell some high-flying terms. The tiles are compiled in specific groups—those groups will appear together in across or down entries.

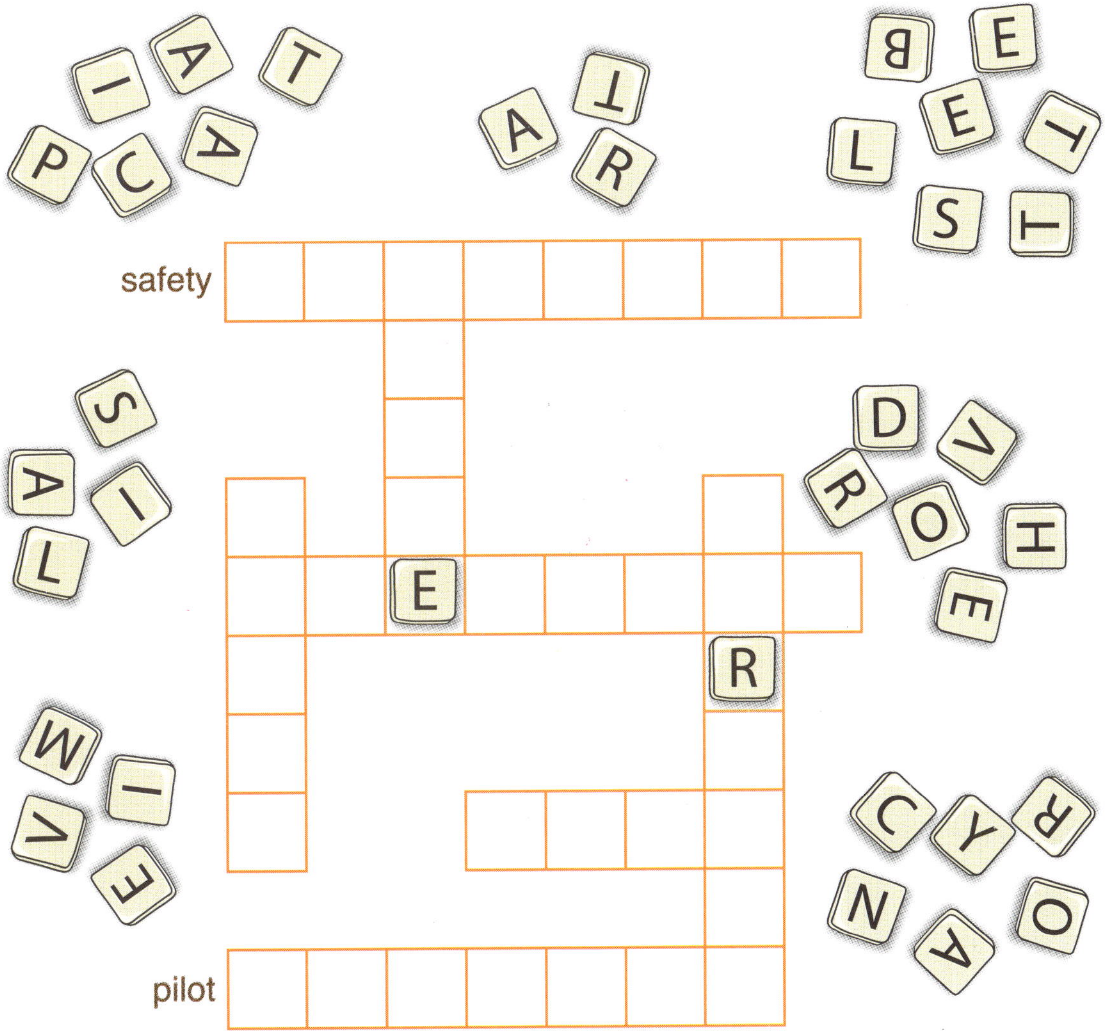

Answer on page 175.

DROP LETTERS

Use all 3 letter tiles to create 4-letter words below.
Each tile will be used once per word.

I K S

R			
		D	
		C	
			P
	N		
		L	

Answer on page 175.

CHAIN WORDS

Place 3 letters in the middle squares that will complete one word and start another. For example, TAR would complete GUI – TAR – GET.

Z	I	P				S	O	N

evel

REWORD REWIND

Unscramble the tiles to form words that will complete the sentence.

R A C T E

In the haunted warehouse, a ☐☐☐☐☐

might vanish without a ☐☐☐☐☐ .

Answers on page 175.

LETTER GRIDLOCK

Use the given tiles to complete the grid with words reading across and down. Use the clues, which are assorted randomly, to help discover the missing words.

CLUES

- Service charge
- Pull hard
- Move smoothly
- Metal container
- Like a geek
- Door opener
- Cow farms
- Burglar
- Blackboard marker
- Argument

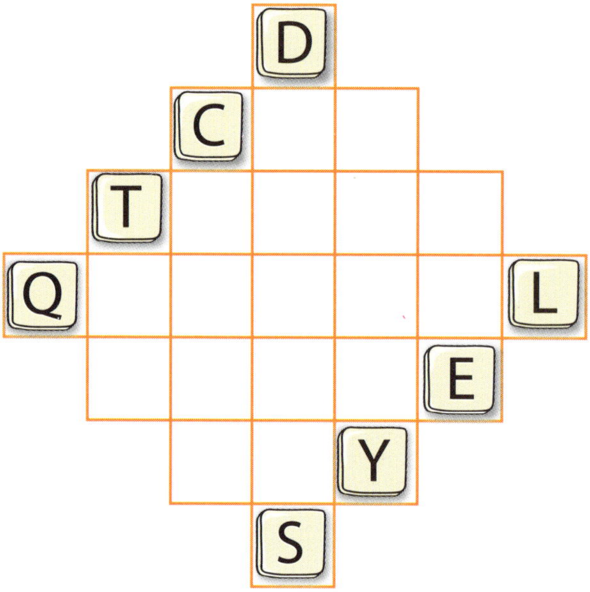

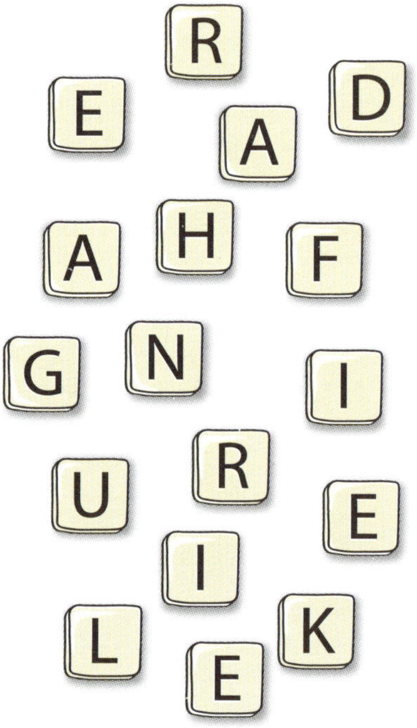

Answer on page 175

REPEAT REPEAT

Use the 8 tiles given to complete each pair of words.
Each pair will use the same 4 letter tiles in the same order.

G L I S

N E A T

		A	P			R
H	O			I		

M		R		A	R			E

S			G			G

Answer on page 175.

ONE UP

Use the 3 tiles at the bottom of the page to solve the bottom clue. Once you do that, move up the page, solving each clue as you go. Carry all the letters used from one clue to the next, rearranging them in the empty spaces.

			T						Units of matter
		P							Exact copies
	C								Cream-filled desserts
	E								Released in regular installments
L									Fibbers
A									Ventilates
									Knight's title

R I S

Answer on page 175

TILE TIE-INS

Using the letter tiles below, complete the grid to reveal 11 characters from "The Simpsons."

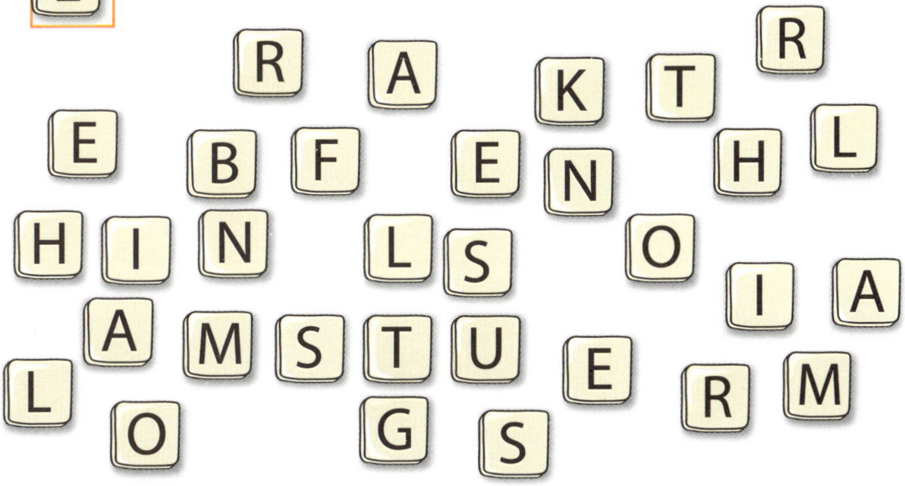

Answer on page 176.

Level

CROSSED OUT

Use the given tiles to spell a pair of related words that meet on the given letter.

					D

E S R

Y O K A

Level

WORD SWATTER

Use 4 letters from the words below to create 4 common words. Letters will be used more than once but will not repeat in each word.

RED SPA

	P			E	
P		D			

	R			E	
S				A	

Answers on page 176

ADD-A-LETTER

Rearrange the tiles from each word, adding one new tile from the bottom in order to form the name of a flower in the empty boxes. Each tile from the bottom of the page is used only once.

O R E	☐ ☐ ☐ ☐
S I R	☐ ☐ ☐ ☐
S A I D	☐ ☐ ☐ ☐ ☐
C A L L	☐ ☐ ☐ ☐ ☐
N O P E	☐ ☐ ☐ ☐ ☐
R A T S	☐ ☐ ☐ ☐ ☐
C H O I R	☐ ☐ ☐ ☐ ☐ ☐

I Y Y D E S I

Answer on page 176.

DROP LETTERS

Use all 3 letter tiles to create 4-letter words below.
Each tile will be used once per word.

E N W

K			
			S
	H		
	A		
A			
S			

Answer on page 176

PILES O' TILES

Place all the tiles into the grid so they spell different types of candy. The tiles are compiled in specific groups—those groups will appear together in across or down entries.

Answer on page 176.

PLUS ONE

Using the letters in the top 3 tiles, create 3 new 4-letter words by adding one of the letters from the bottom 3 tiles.

S I T

F E K

P A N

W L T

Answer on page 176

LETTER GRIDLOCK

Use the given tiles to complete the grid with words reading across and down. Use the clues, which are assorted randomly, to help discover the missing words.

CLUES

- Alabama or Alaska
- Bother
- Boy's name (hidden in "awesome")
- Brown songbirds
- Full of envy
- Hopping mad
- Land of St. Patrick
- Letters that follow ems
- Take to court
- Tie them in a rope

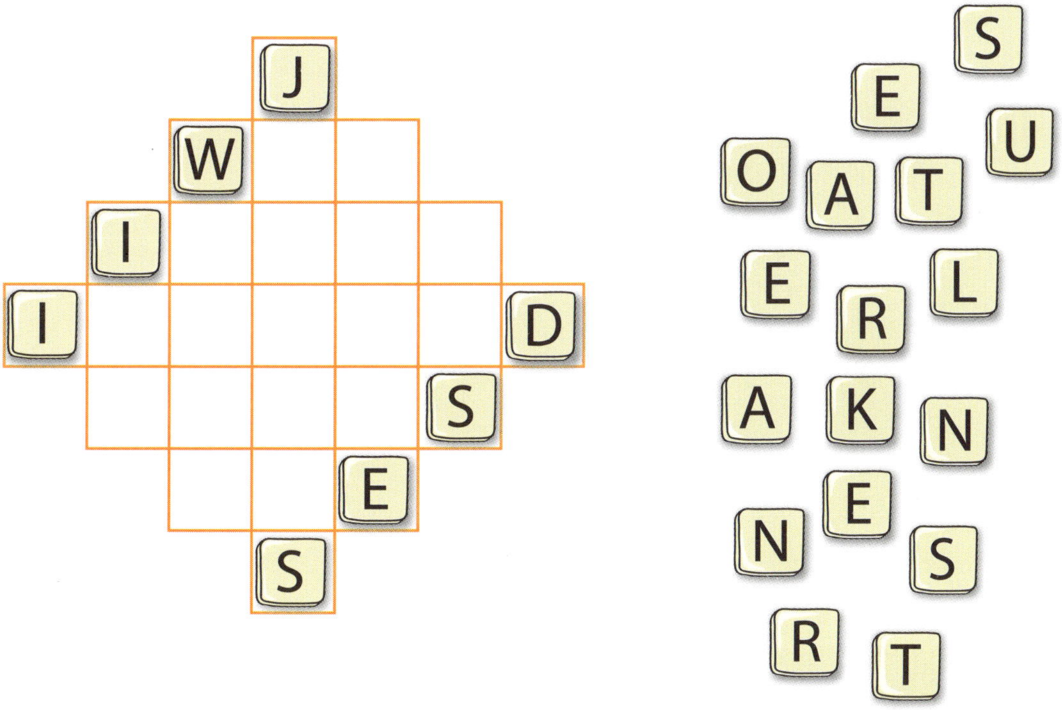

Answer on page 176.

COME TOGETHER

Place each of the tile sets into the empty spaces below to create 3 nine-letter birds. Each tile set is used only once.

S A P   D E E   A L B

S U C   O S S   C H I

K E R   C K A   A T R

Answer on page 176.

REWORD REWIND

Unscramble the tiles to form words that will complete the sentence.

The letter I ☐☐☐☐

started "☐☐☐☐ David."

A R D E

Level

CHAIN WORDS

Place 3 letters in the middle squares that will complete one word and start another. For example, TAR would complete GUI – TAR – GET.

S O C ☐ ☐ ☐ E A L

Answers on pages 176–177.

WORD STICKERS

Use the letter tiles given to complete the word pairs. Each pair of words will be a homonym (words that sound alike, but are spelled differently) of one another.

E T I
Y M T E

		M	

	H			

D B D A
N B N

	A		

		N		E	

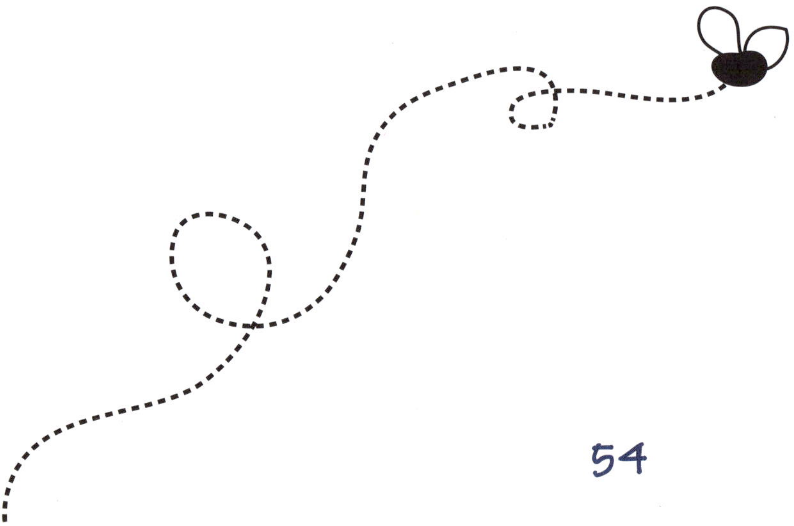

Answer on page 177.

THEME PARK

This "ride" has a theme, but we can't tell you what it is. Place all the words in the boxes below—when you do, read the word created in the outlined boxes, from top to bottom, to reveal what the theme is.

BOOTS	HAT	SCARF
COAT	JACKET	SWEATER
EARMUFFS	LONG UNDERWEAR	WOOL SOCKS
GLOVES	MITTENS	

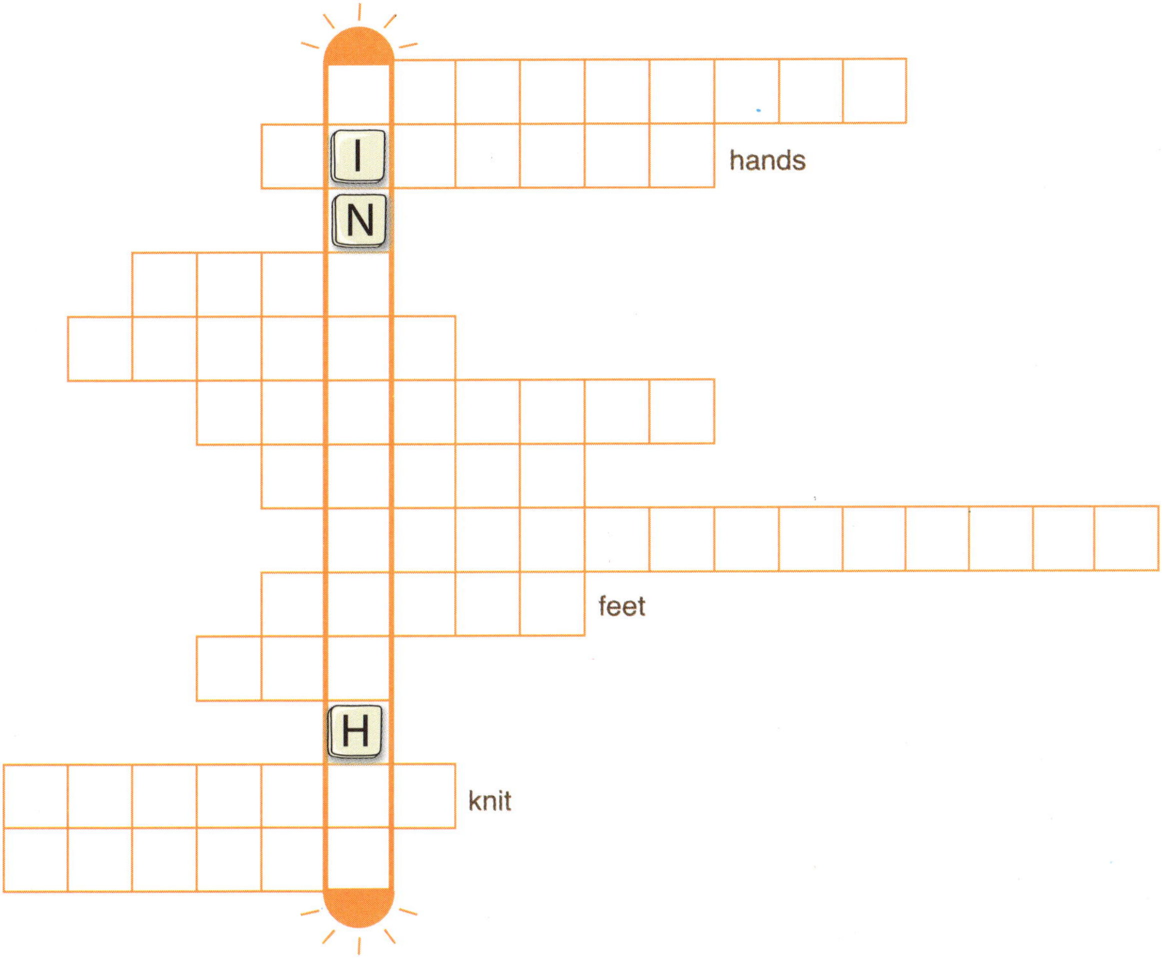

Answer on page 177.

CRUNCHED LETTERS

Create 3 words by placing the letter tiles into the grid. Two tiles will be added to the 3-letter sets given—one letter at the beginning and another at the end.

	E	C	A	
	E	C	A	
	E	C	A	

P P L R N D

Answer on page 177

FITTING TILES

In this miniature crossword, the clues are listed randomly. It is up to you to figure out the placement of the 9 answers. To help you, we've inserted 2 letters in the grid, and this is the only occurrence of those letters in the completed puzzle.

CLUES

- Opposite of take
- Bottoms of shoes
- Sound from a horse
- Short afternoon sleeps
- Object that gets worshiped
- _____-visual
- Gardening tools
- Show to be true
- Money in France or Spain

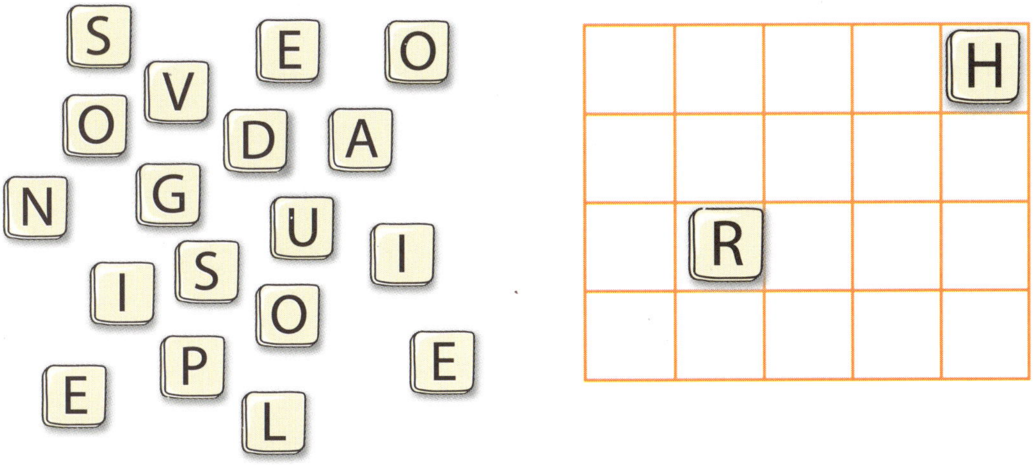

Answer on page 177.

ONE UP

Use the 3 tiles at the bottom of the page to solve the bottom clue. Once you do that, move up the page, solving each clue as you go. Carry all the letters used from one clue to the next, rearranging them in the empty spaces.

Grid	Clue
_ A _ _ _ _ _ _ _	Citrus fruit
_ _ _ _ _ _ N _	Going in
_ _ _ _ G _ _	Whole number
_ N _ _ _ _	Whole
_ E _ _ _	Do up laces again
_ _ _ R	Wedding cake layer
_ _ _	Do up laces

I E T

Answer on page 177

SHUFFLE BOARD

Rearrange each of the letters in the words below to form new words. Place the new words into the grid. One letter has already been placed.

ABET GAB

ARE PAGED

BALED RATED

B				

Gecko-pedia

There's only one English word that begins and ends with the letters "und." You may think you'll come out on top if you know the answer, but really, what you're looking for is "underground."

Answer on page 177.

WORD SWATTER

Use 3 letters from the words below to create 10 common words. Letters will be used more than once but will not repeat in each word.

T H E S U N

	U							T
		S				U		
		N			H			
		T					U	
	H							E

Level

JUMBLED UP

Place each letter into the empty boxes below to create a common word. Tiles are in the correct order, but they are not in the upright position.

F R E E Z E

Answers on page 17

REPEAT REPEAT

Use the 8 tiles given to complete each pair of words.
Each pair will use the same 4 letter tiles in the same order.

E	P	R	C
I	O	S	N

P		N			L	
R				P	E	

	P			C	O			
	F	F	S			I		G

Answer on page 178.

ADD-A-LETTER

Rearrange the tiles from each word, adding one new tile from the bottom in order to form the name of a color in the empty boxes. Each tile from the bottom of the page is used only once.

K I N ☐☐☐☐

L O G ☐☐☐☐

G E N E ☐☐☐☐☐

W I T H ☐☐☐☐☐

W O R N ☐☐☐☐☐

R A G ☐☐☐☐

R E Y P B D

Answer on page 17

LETTER GRIDLOCK

Use the given tiles to complete the grid with words reading across and down. Use the clues, which are assorted randomly, to help discover the missing words.

CLUES

- Baseball player's hat
- Copy on paper
- Cricket sound
- Dog or goldfish, often
- Freshly painted
- Pitch or pass
- Pixie dust producers
- Took as husband or wife
- Water faucet
- Writing end of a pencil

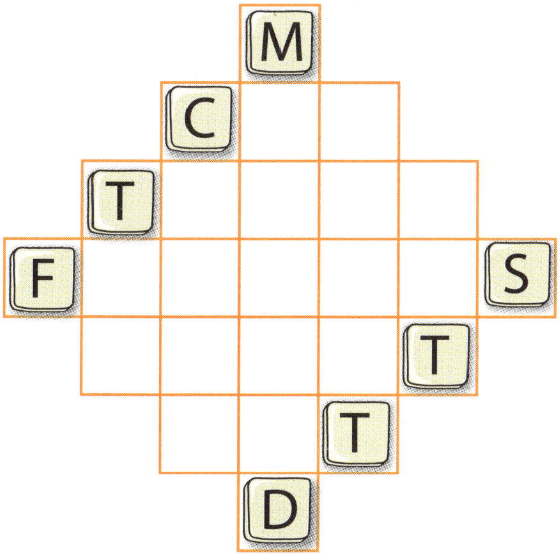

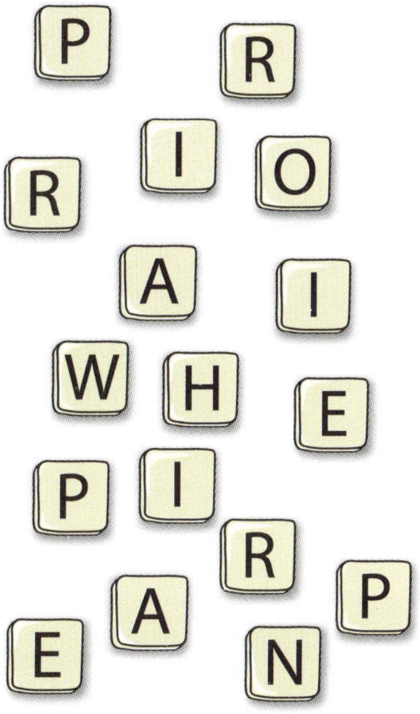

Answer on page 178.

CROSSED OUT

Use the given tiles to spell a pair of related words that meet on the given letter.

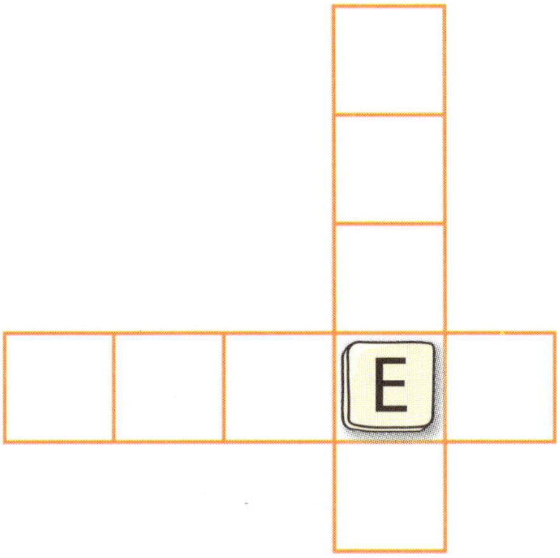

H T R R

Y I P D

Gecko-pedia

Each of the 25 most-often-used verbs only has one syllable. Top of the list? "Be."

Answer on page 178

TILE TIE-INS

Using the letter tiles below, complete the grid to reveal 9 words from the Pledge of Allegiance.

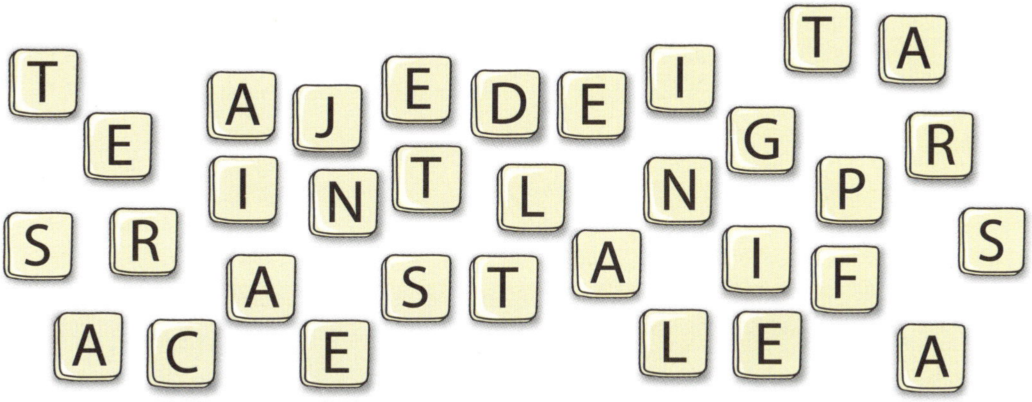

Answer on page 178.

PILES O' TILES

Place all the tiles into the grid so they spell "spacey" words. The tiles are compiled in specific groups—those groups will appear together in across or down entries.

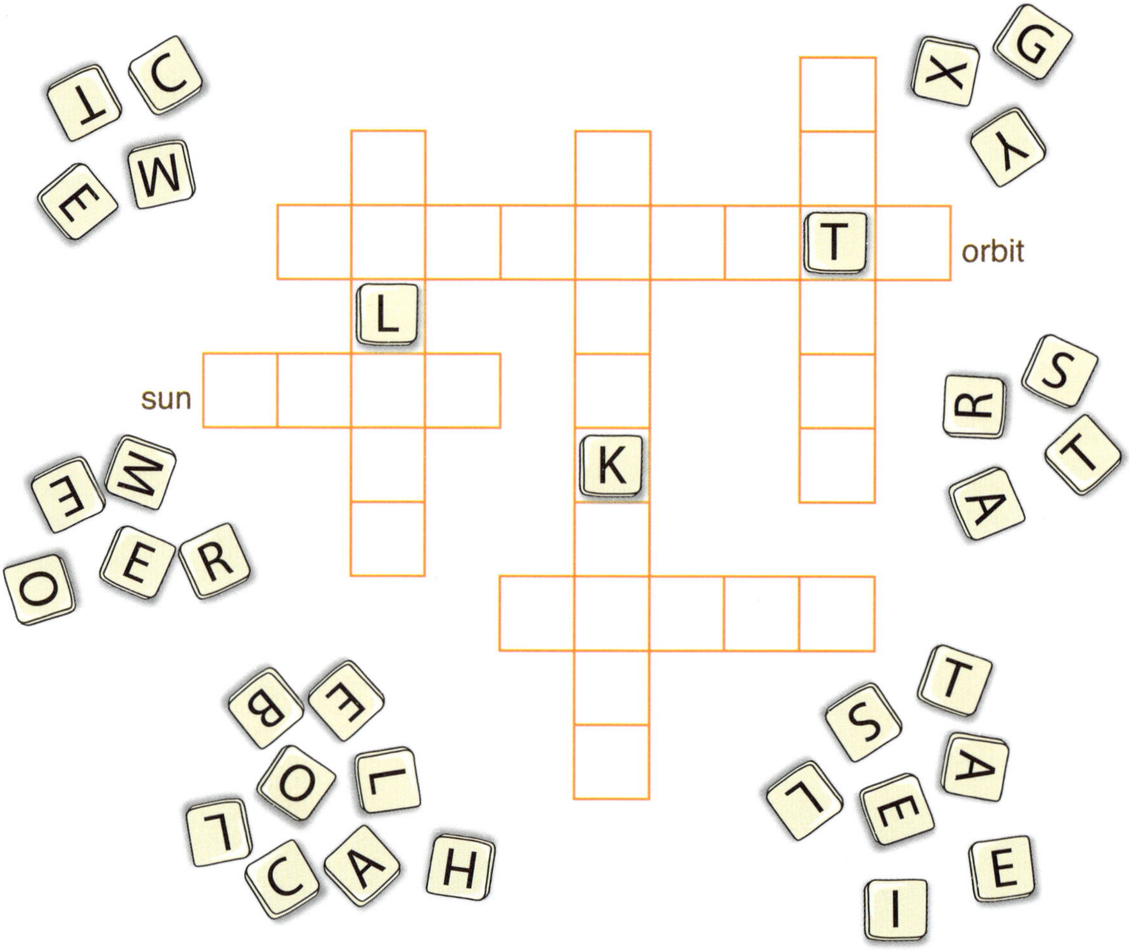

Answer on page 178

DROP LETTERS

Use all 3 letter tiles to create 4-letter words below.
Each tile will be used once per word.

A T P

		S	
			H
S			
	I		
		O	
		N	

Answer on page 178.

FITTING TILES

In this miniature crossword, the clues are listed randomly. It is up to you to figure out the placement of the 9 answers. To help you, we've inserted 2 letters in the grid, and this is the only occurrence of those letters in the completed puzzle.

CLUES

- Water vapor from a kettle
- Ten "little piggies" on your feet
- Break out of an eggshell
- Singing voice in a choir
- They give parties
- Meats sliced at delis
- Greeting in Hawaii
- Talk with a friend
- Corned beef dish

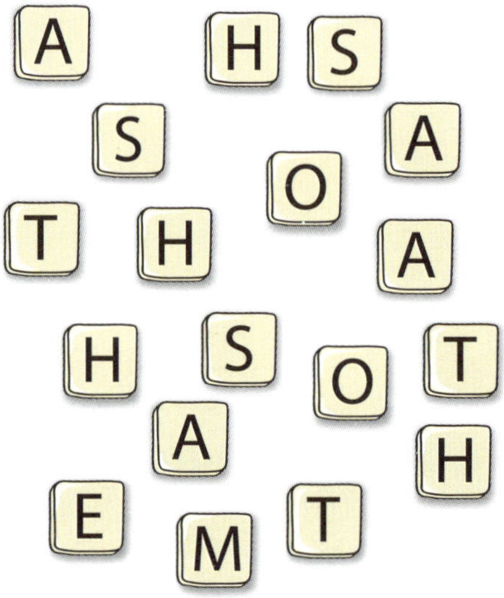

			C	
	L			

Answer on page 178

ONE UP

Use the 3 tiles at the bottom of the page to solve the bottom clue. Once you do that, move up the page, solving each clue as you go. Carry all the letters used from one clue to the next, rearranging them in the empty spaces.

_ _ _ _ _ _ _ _ G	Practicing drawing
_ _ _ _ _ _ _ S	Cooking rooms
_ _ _ _ K _ _	Become more dense
_ T _ _ _ _	Of a culture
_ _ _ H _	Alcove
N _ _ _	Pleasant
_ _ _	Frozen water

E C I

Answer on page 179.

WORD STICKERS

Use the letter tiles given to complete the word pairs.
Each pair of words will be an antonym (opposite) of one another.

L B E
E O O A

	B		V	

				W

L Y T U
L E M

		P		

F			

You know what the opposite of antonym is? Synonym! Synonyms are words that mean the same thing.

Answer on page 179

ALPHABET EXPRESS

Use every letter tile below to complete the grid with common words.

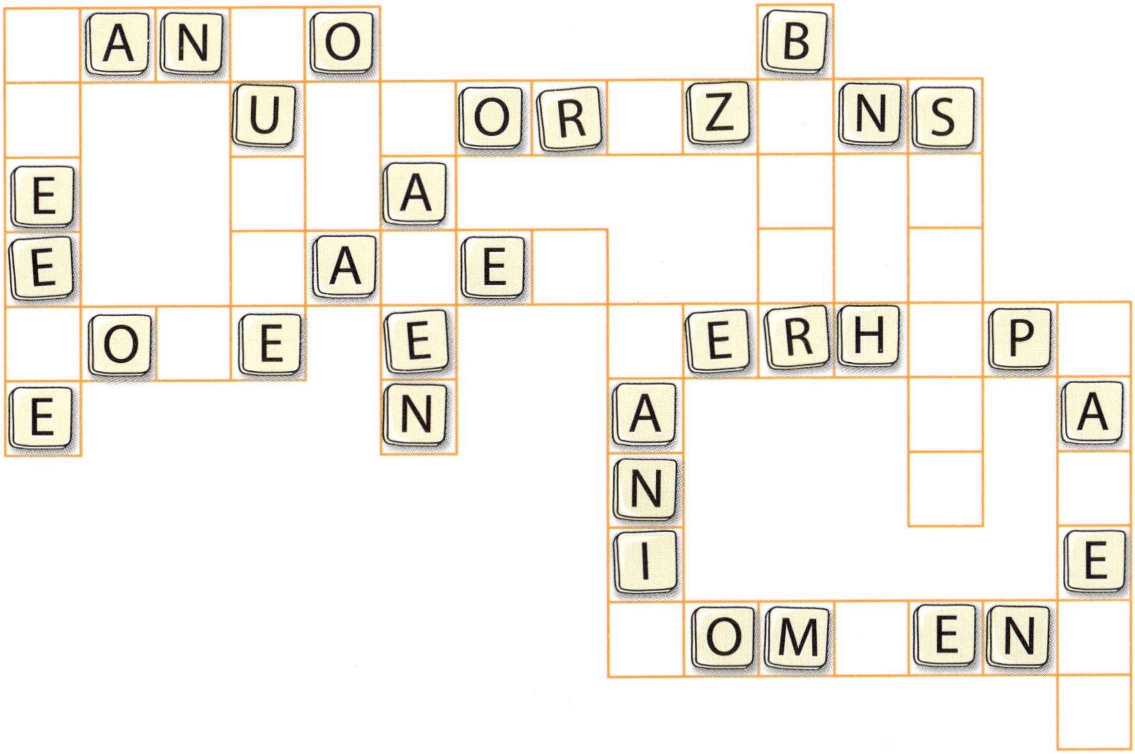

A B C D E F G H I

J K L M N O P Q

R S T U V W X Y Z

Answer on page 179.

SHUFFLE BOARD

Rearrange each of the letters in the words below to form new words. Place the new words into the grid. One letter has already been placed.

F A T E   S E A T S

S A F E R   S T A K E

T H U S

		K		

Gecko-pedia

There are only 4 English words with a double-u: "vacuum," "continuum," "muumuu," and "residuum." Check out "muumuu"—it's got a double-double-u!

Answer on page 179

PLUS ONE

Using the letters in the top 3 tiles, create 3 new 4-letter words by adding one of the letters from the bottom 3 tiles.

G E E

N L K

H A D

S E R

Answer on page 179.

ADD-A-LETTER

Rearrange the tiles from each word, adding one new tile from the bottom in order to form a vegetable in the empty boxes. Each tile from the bottom of the page is used only once.

S A N E

A P E

C H A I N S

B E S T

R O C

P R I N T S

N O O N S

I N S U P B E

Answer on page 179

COME TOGETHER

Place each of the tile sets into the empty spaces below to create 3 nine-letter American cities. Each tile set is used only once.

M I L	T E R	W A U
K E E	A N D	R O C
H E S	V E L	C L E

Answer on page 179.

CRUNCHED LETTERS

Create 3 words by placing the letter tiles into the grid. Two tiles will be added to the 3-letter sets given—one letter at the beginning and another at the end.

	A	N	O	
	A	N	O	
	A	N	O	

R E N C M C

Level

REWORD REWIND

Unscramble the tiles to form words that will complete the sentence.

The athlete wanted to ____ for shoes to make her ____ and leaps higher.

O S P H

Answers on page 179

THEME PARK

This "ride" has a theme, but we can't tell you what it is. Place all the words in the boxes below—when you do, read the word created in the outlined boxes, from top to bottom, to reveal what the theme is.

ASTEROID	MERCURY	SUN
EARTH	MOON	URANUS
JUPITER	PLUTO	VENUS
MARS	SATURN	

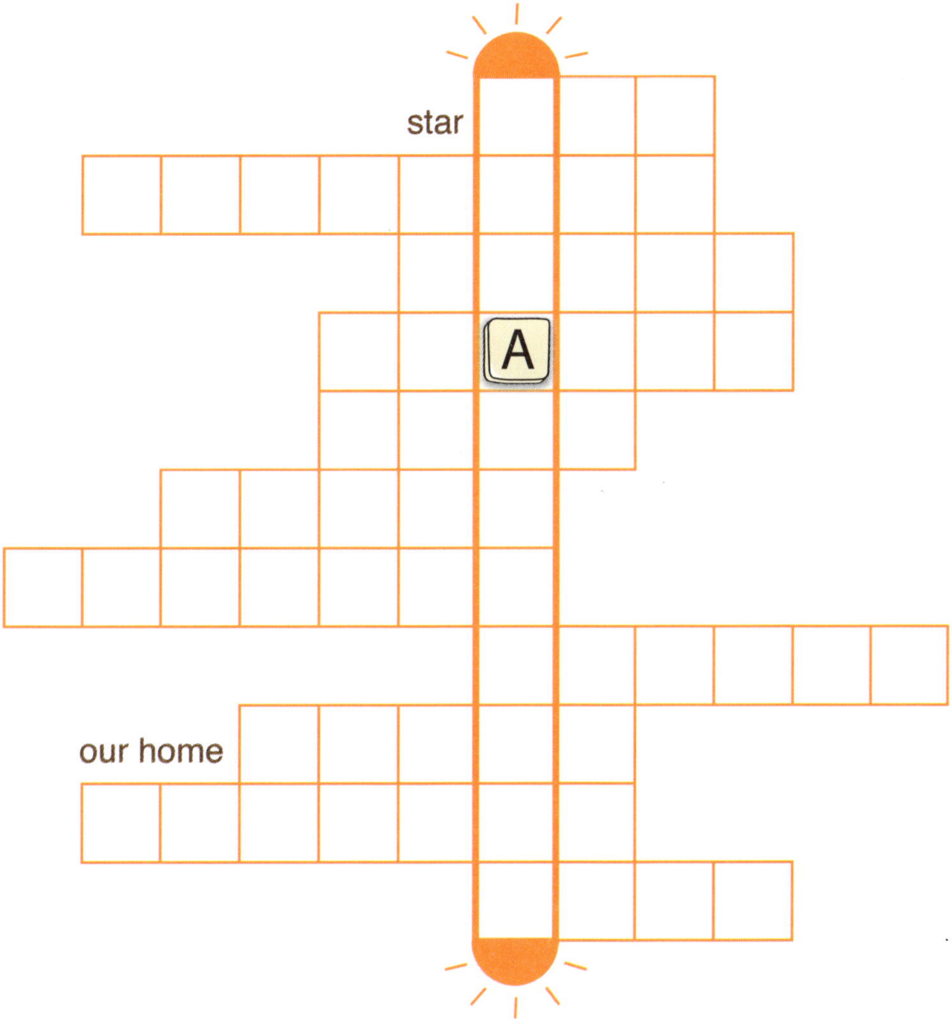

Answer on page 180.

TILE TIE-INS

Using the letter tiles below, complete the grid to reveal 10 different languages.

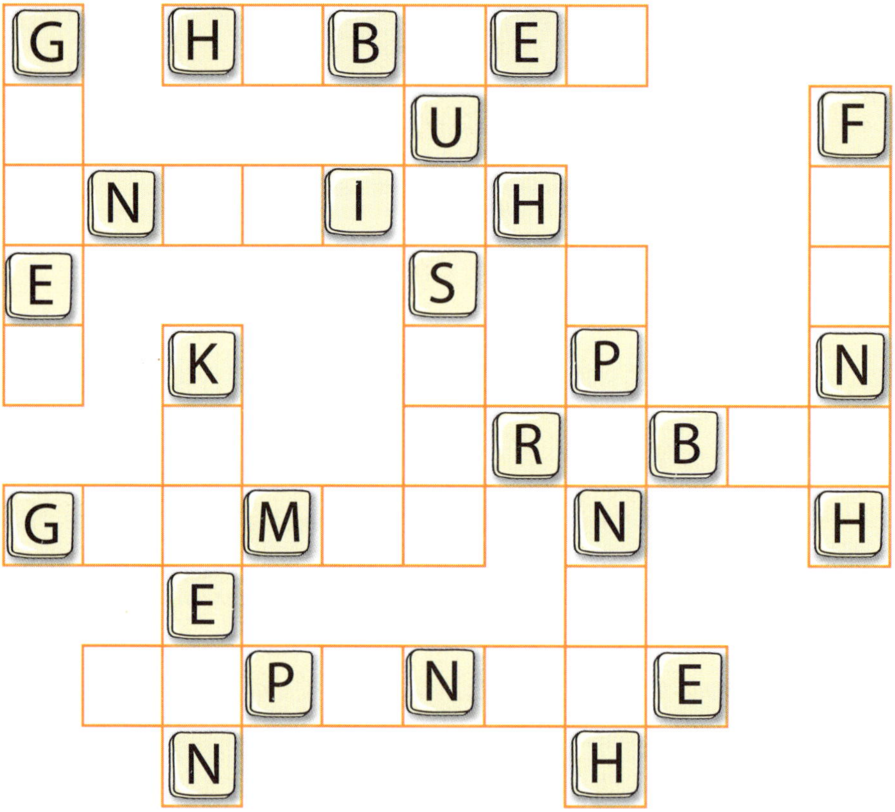

Answer on page 18C

LETTER GRIDLOCK

Use the given tiles to complete the grid with words reading across and down. Use the clues, which are assorted randomly, to help discover the missing words.

CLUES

- Under
- Type of bear
- Prepared for action
- Pig residence
- More elegant
- In favor of
- Listlessness
- Electrical lines
- Drenched
- Boy's name (hidden in "destroyer")

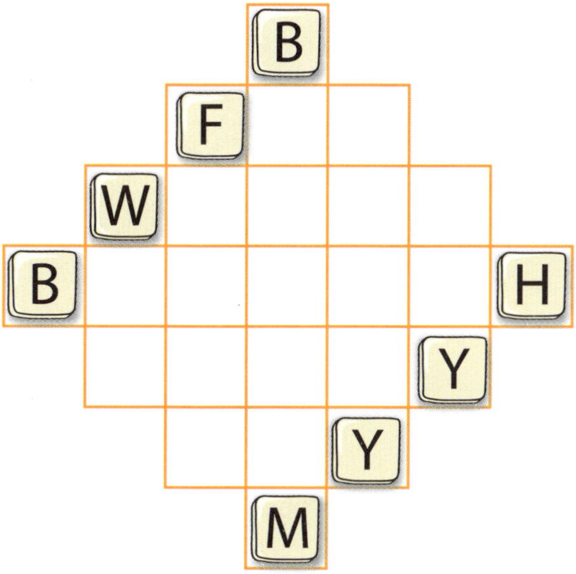

Answer on page 180.

ONE UP

Use the 3 tiles at the bottom of the page to solve the bottom clue. Once you do that, move up the page, solving each clue as you go. Carry all the letters used from one clue to the next, rearranging them in the empty spaces.

							N		Puts in danger
		E							Movie houses
			T						Break into small pieces
					S				Valentine shapes
		R							Third rock from the sun
	E								Warmth
									Head topper

A T H

Answer on page 180

REPEAT REPEAT

Use the 8 tiles given to complete each pair of words.
Each pair will use the same 4 letter tiles in the same order.

P L C E
R O S I

B			Y	C		

T			K		

		W	D	E		

S				T	

Answer on page 180.

TILE TIE-INS

Using the letter tiles below, complete the grid to reveal 10 types of seafood.

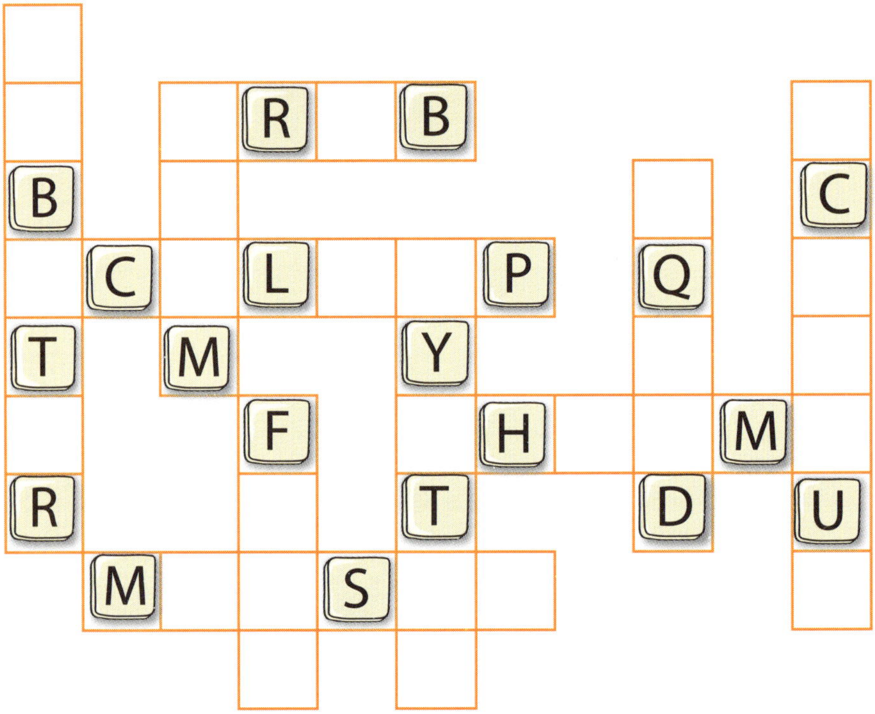

Answer on page 180

CROSSED OUT

Use the given tiles to spell a pair of related words that meet on the given letter.

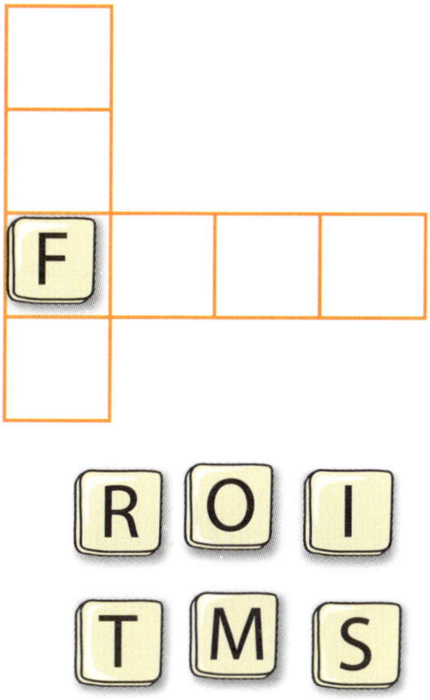

evel

CHAIN WORDS

Place 2 letters in the middle squares that will complete one word and start another. For example, ER would complete FLI – ER – ROR.

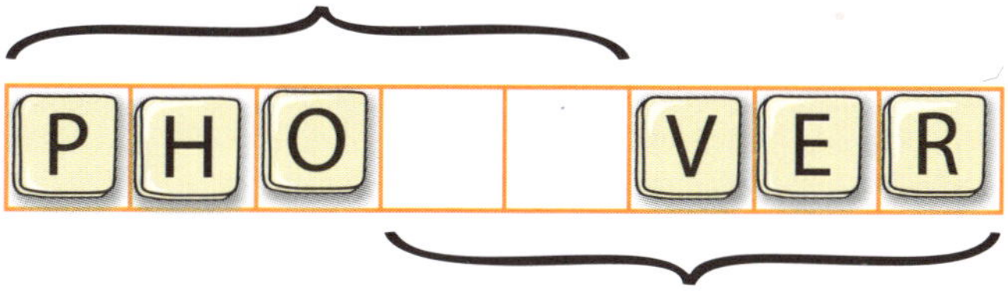

Answers on pages 180–181.

COME TOGETHER

Place each of the tile sets into the empty spaces below to create 3 nine-letter comic book heroes. Each tile set is used only once.

S P I	D A R	I N E
E D E	V I L	D E R
V E R	M A N	W O L

Answer on page 18

PLUS ONE

Using the letters in the top 3 tiles, create 3 new 4-letter words by adding one of the letters from the bottom 3 tiles.

T A P

R E S

T O T

R U E

If you get stuck, try testing out different word combos with the tiles and see what works!

Answer on page 181.

WORD SWATTER

Use 3 letters from the words below to create 6 common words. Letters will be used more than once but will not repeat in each word.

S E A   C O W

	W		
A			
	C		

W			
	O		
C			

Level

REWORD REWIND

Unscramble the tiles to form words that will complete the sentence.

I went to the store for a ☐☐☐☐☐ for the iced tea and a ☐☐☐☐☐ for the fruit salad.

M E N L O

Answers on page 18

LETTER GRIDLOCK

Use the given tiles to complete the grid with words reading across and down. Use the clues, which are assorted randomly, to help discover the missing words.

CLUES

- Go for a target
- Hospital departments
- Accomplished
- Dried with a towel
- Hopelessness
- Mix thoroughly
- Purpose
- Spider's home
- Use them to close your clothes
- Walkway in a theater

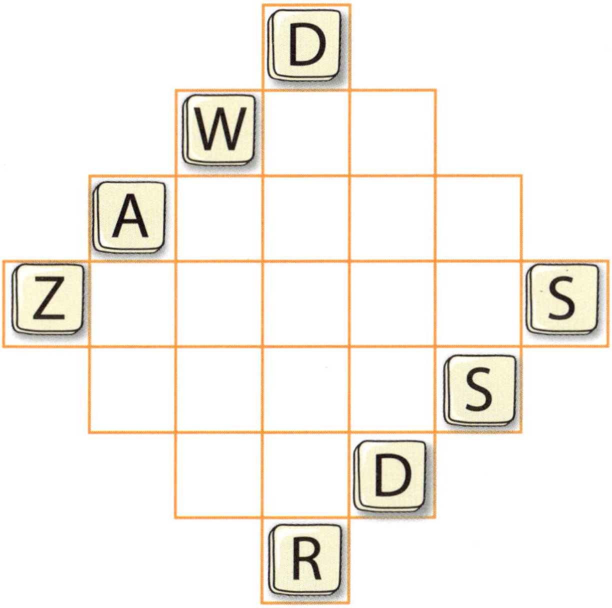

Answer on page 181.

PILES O' TILES

Place all the tiles into the grid so they spell a jungle of safari-themed words. The tiles are compiled in specific groups—those groups will appear together in across or down entries.

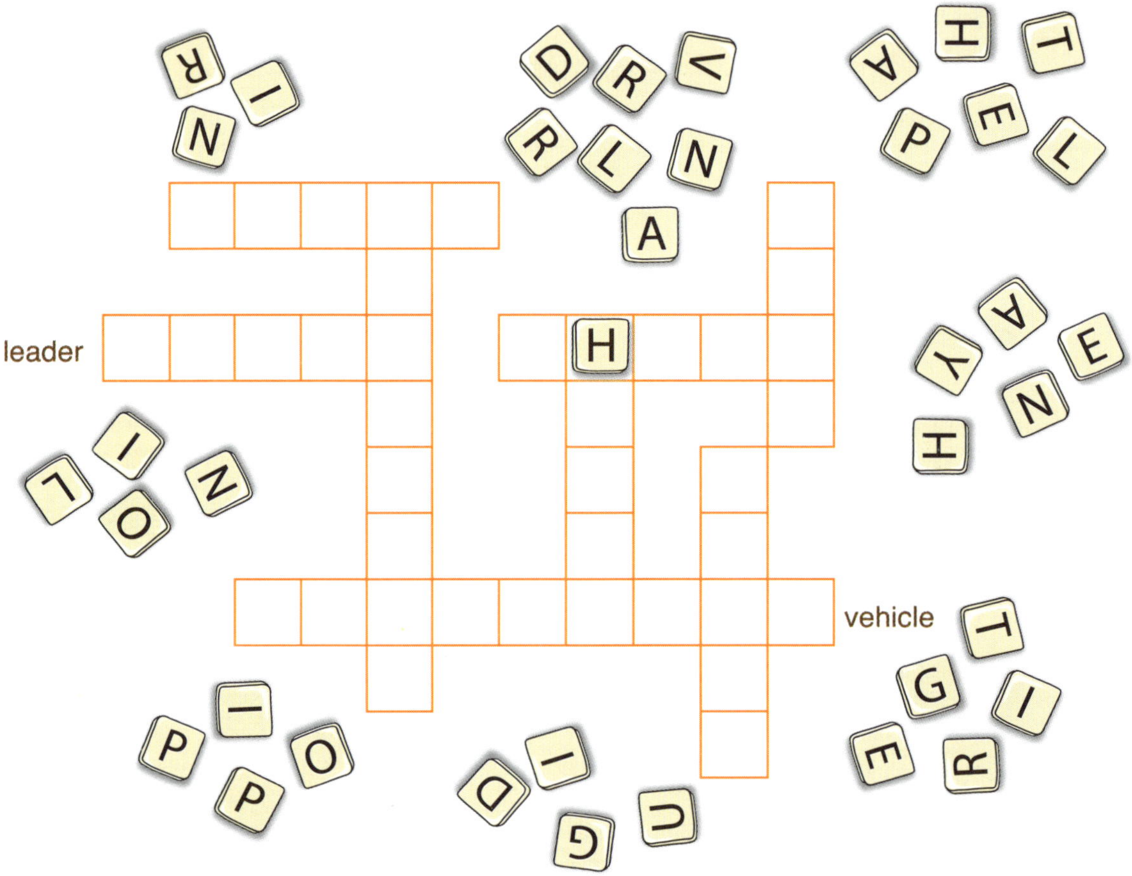

Answer on page 18

ALPHABET EXPRESS

Use every letter tile below to complete the grid with common words.

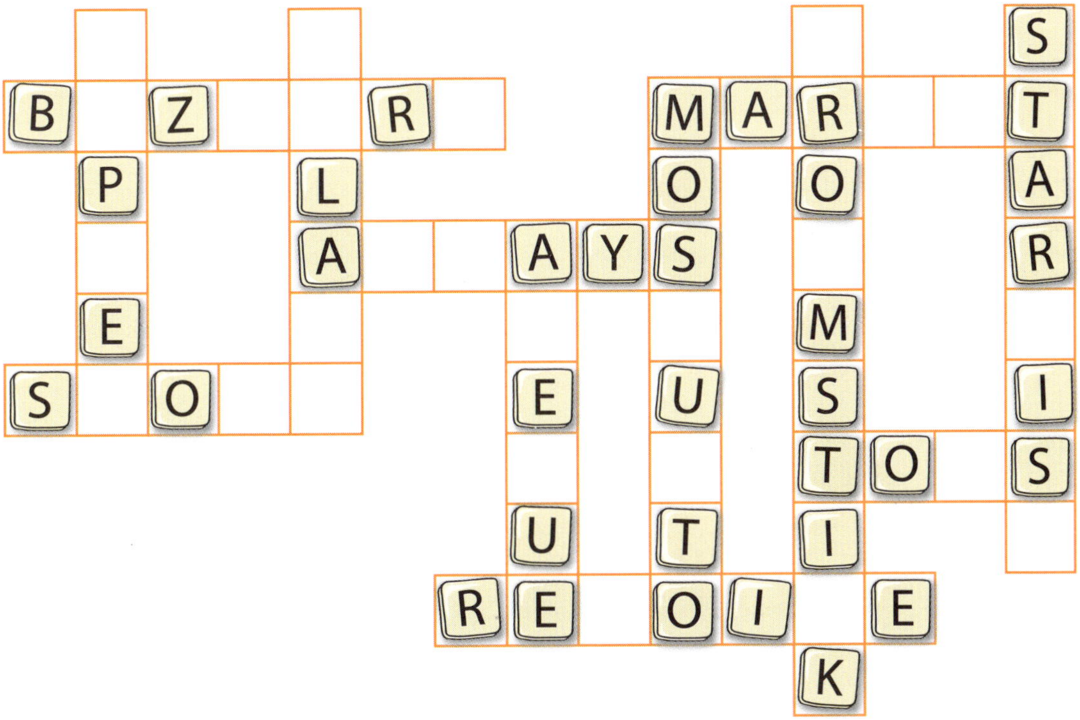

Answer on page 181.

FITTING TILES

In this miniature crossword, the clues are listed randomly. It is up to you to figure out the placement of the 9 answers. To help you, we've inserted 2 letters in the grid, and this is the only occurrence of those letters in the completed puzzle.

CLUES

- Large country with a city called Mumbai
- Grain thrown at weddings
- Closed hand
- Tinkerbell was one
- Big, shaggy animals in Tibet
- Bathroom floor squares
- Singing superstar
- New York _____ Exchange
- Against

F				
				K

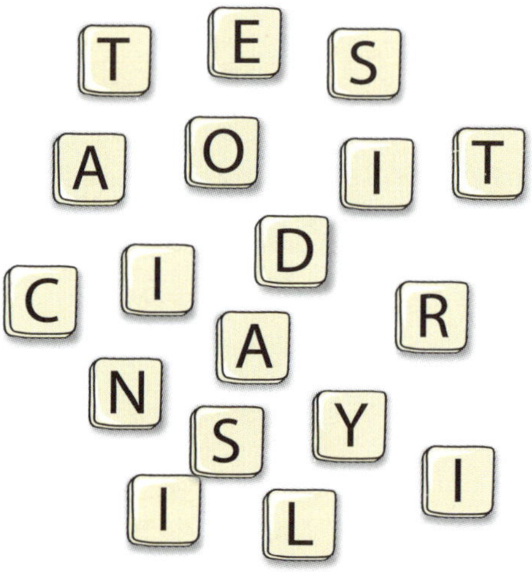

Answer on page 181

ADD-A-LETTER

Rearrange the tiles from each word, adding one new tile from the bottom in order to form a sound you may hear in a haunted house. Each tile from the bottom of the page is used only once.

S M E A R

R A C K

R A N G

C H A R

G A B

C H A R T S

W I P E R S

E O S H C N C

Answer on page 182.

THEME PARK

This "ride" has a theme, but we can't tell you what it is. Place all the words in the boxes below—when you do, read the word created in the outlined boxes, from top to bottom, to reveal what the theme is.

CALL	LOL
CASE	PARENTS
EMERGENCY	RINGTONE
FRIENDS	TEXTING
HOME	

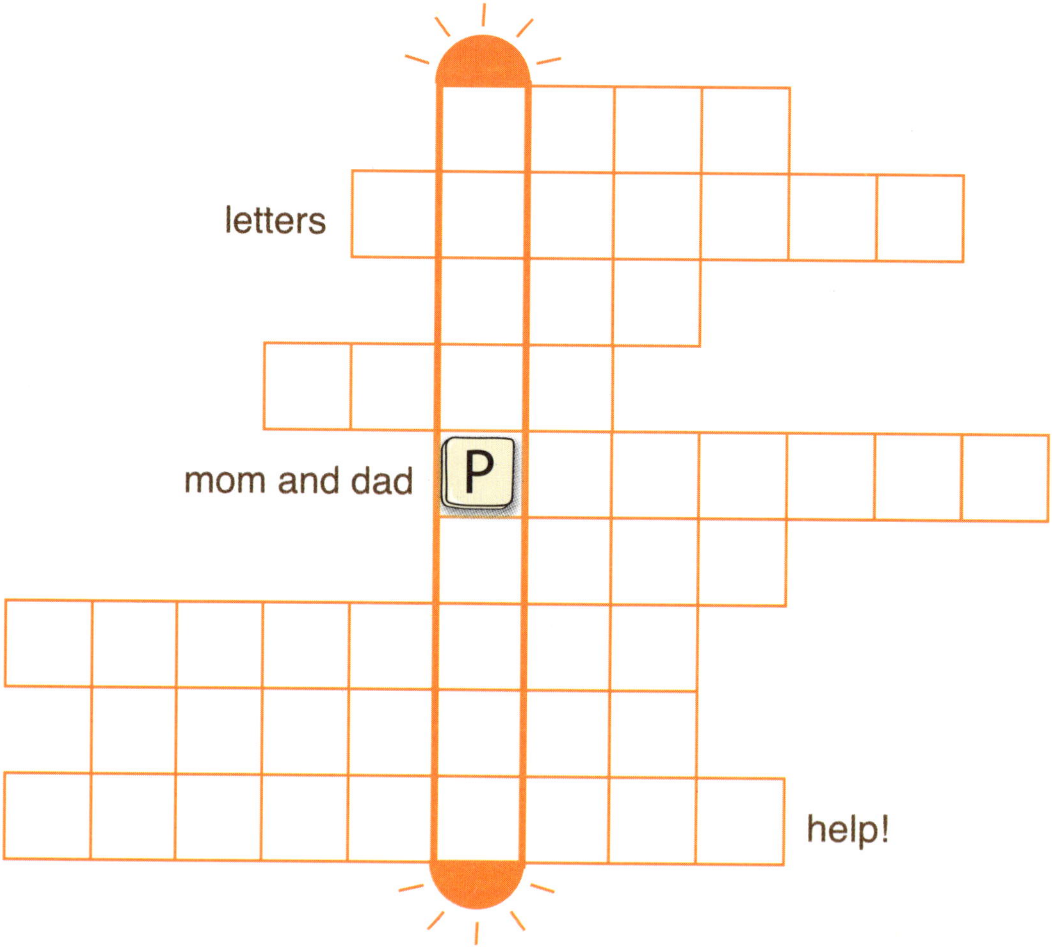

Answer on page 182

DROP LETTERS

Use all 3 letter tiles to create 4-letter words below.
Each tile will be used once per word.

C E H

	A		

			W

			O

A			

			F

	T		

Gecko-pedia

Anagrams aren't only about fun and games. Doctors use them to test some areas of a person's memory as well, a function that comes in handy with patients who have amnesia.

Answer on page 182.

SHUFFLE BOARD

Rearrange each of the letters in the words below to form new words. Place the new words into the grid. One letter has already been placed.

LEAP ROOTS

PLATE SPOT

RIA STALE

Level

REWORD REWIND

Unscramble the tiles to form words that will complete the sentence.

The truck driver hauling pots and ☐☐☐☐ took

some ☐☐☐☐ to get rest before crossing

bridges that ☐☐☐☐ the Mississippi River.

A P N S

Answers on page 182

CRUNCHED LETTERS

Create 3 words by placing the letter tiles into the grid. Two tiles will be added to the 3-letter sets given—one letter at the beginning and another at the end.

evel

CHAIN WORDS

Place 3 letters in the middle squares that will complete one word and start another. For example, TAR would complete GUI – TAR – GET.

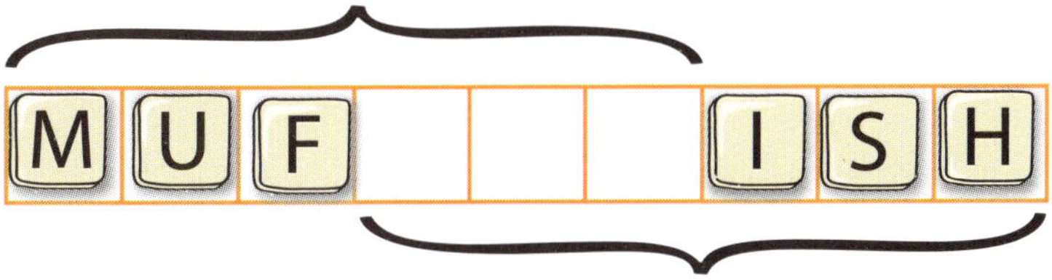

Answers on page 182.

COME TOGETHER

Place each of the tile sets into the empty spaces below to create 3 nine-letter U.S. states. Each tile set is used only once.

TEN   MEX   SIN

WIS   SEE   NES

NEW   ICO   CON

Answer on page 182

PILES O' TILES

Place all the tiles into the grid so they spell a rainbow of words. The tiles are compiled in specific groups—those groups will appear together in across or down entries.

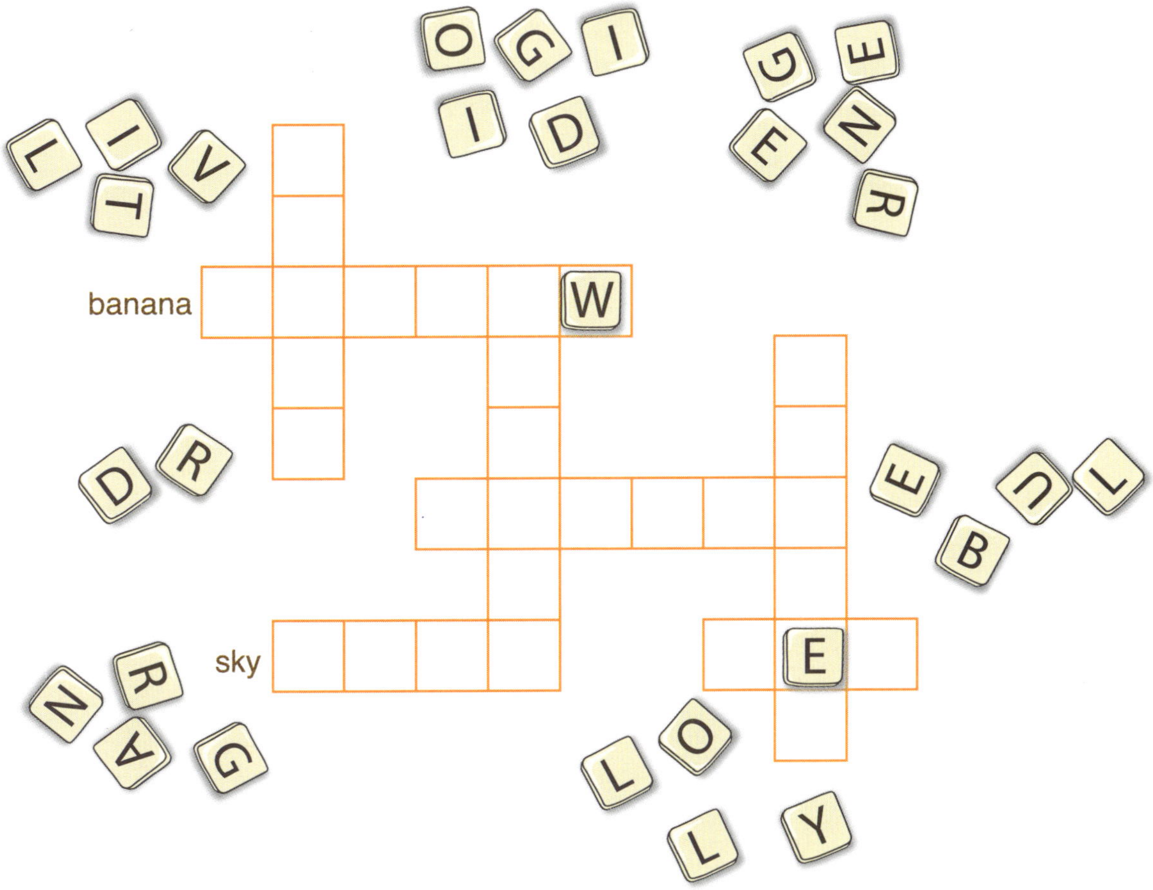

Answer on page 182.

REPEAT REPEAT

Use the 8 tiles given to complete each pair of words.
Each pair will use the same 4 letter tiles in the same order.

G E T A

U L I R

R		S		A		R		N	T

P				N	I	

	A				C

	I				E

Answer on page 182

ONE UP

Use the 3 tiles at the bottom of the page to solve the bottom clue. Once you do that, move up the page, solving each clue as you go. Carry all the letters used from one clue to the next, rearranging them in the empty spaces.

_ _ _ A _ _ _ _ _ ...... Seek vengeance

_ _ _ _ _ A _ _ ...... Able to read and write

_ E _ _ _ _ _ ...... Give a new name

_ _ T _ _ _ ...... Drop garbage

_ _ _ _ R ...... Metric measure

T _ _ _ ...... Piece of bathroom wall

_ _ _ ...... Falsehood

E I L

Answer on page 183.

ALPHABET EXPRESS

Use every letter tile below to complete the grid with common words.

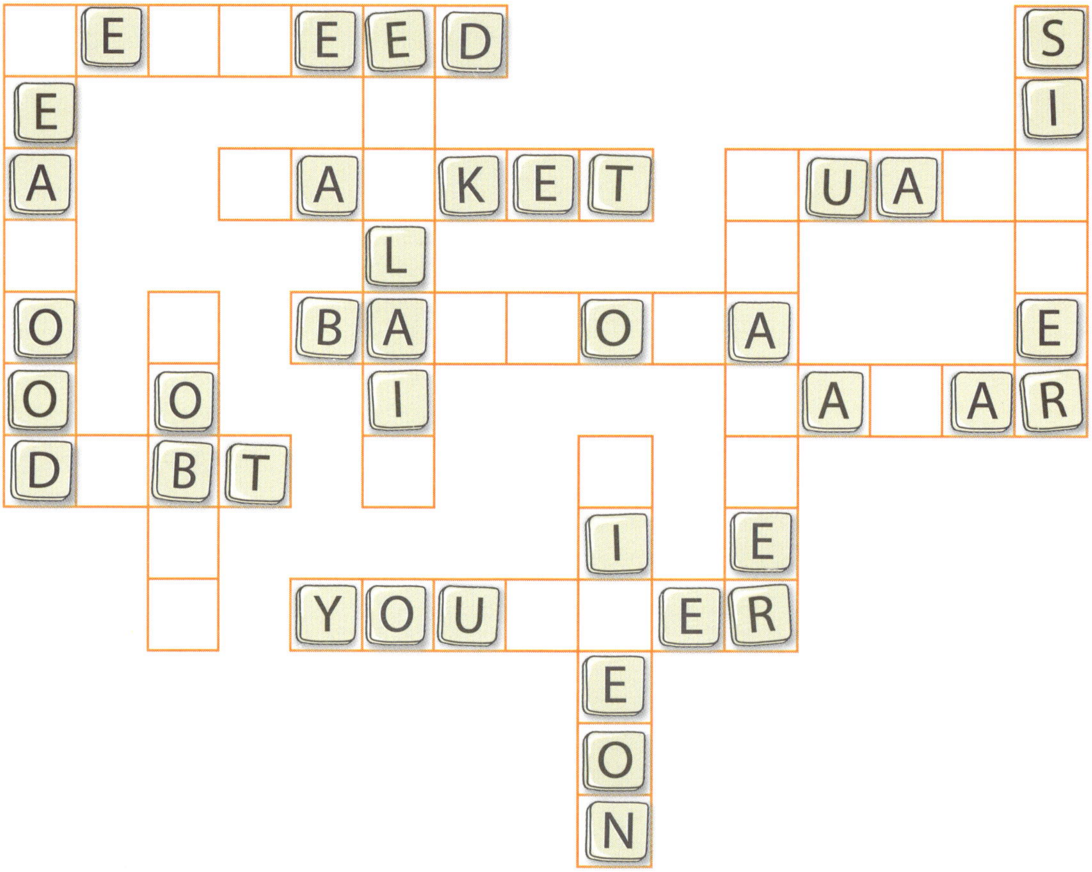

A B C D E F G H I

J K L M N O P Q

R S T U V W X Y Z

Answer on page 183

WORD STICKERS

Use the letter tiles given to complete the word pairs. Each pair of words will be a synonym (words with similar meanings) of one another.

A T D S
O L N S

		O			E	

P				A

E C L
R I O C

				K

T		M		

Answer on page 183.

LETTER GRIDLOCK

Use the given tiles to complete the grid with words reading across and down. Use the clues, which are assorted randomly, to help discover the missing words.

CLUES

- Win
- Tied up, like sneakers
- Ripped off
- Paintings and drawings
- Hold in
- Gave out the cards
- Christmas visitor
- Boy's name (hidden in "beside")
- Bite the dust
- ___ Angeles, California

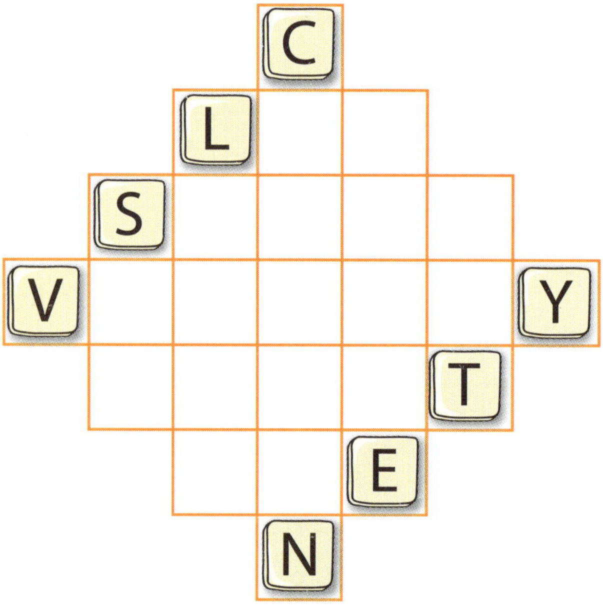

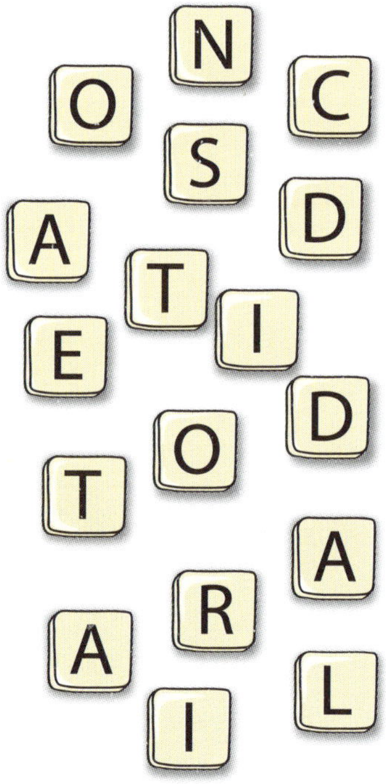

Answer on page 183

PLUS ONE

Using the letters in the top 3 tiles, create 3 new 4-letter words by adding one of the letters from the bottom 3 tiles.

B U T

S O N

M A N

O I Y

Answer on page 183.

TILE TIE-INS

Using the letter tiles below, complete the grid to reveal 9 types of cooking spices.

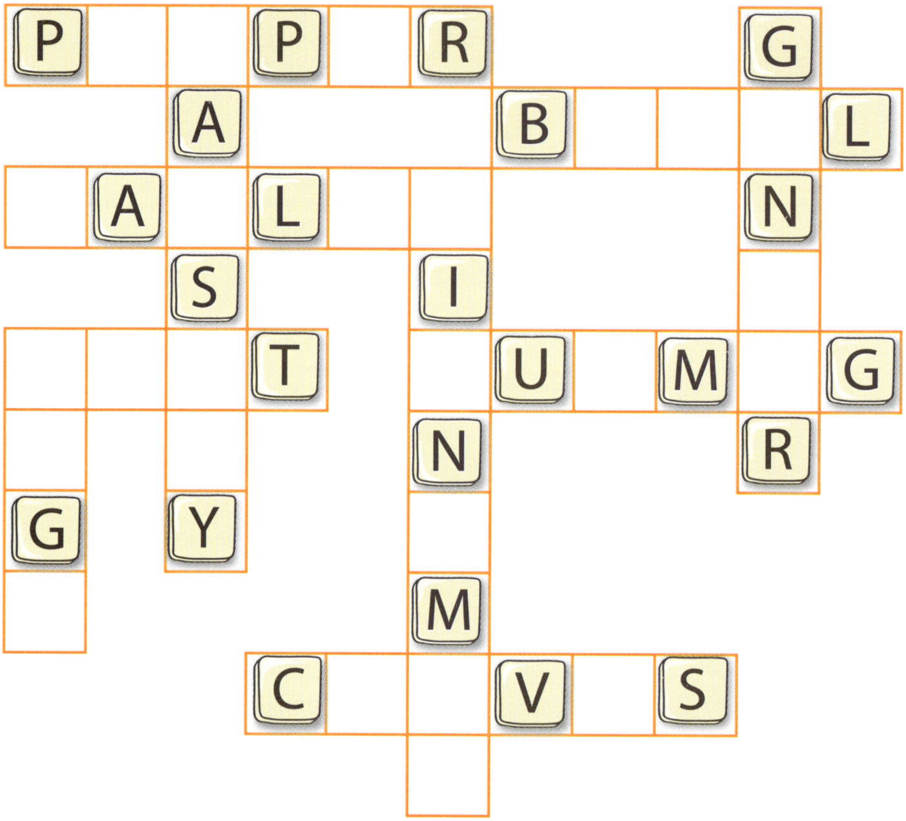

Answer on page 183

PILES O' TILES

Place all the tiles into the grid so they spell some camping-related words. The tiles are compiled in specific groups—those groups will appear together in across or down entries.

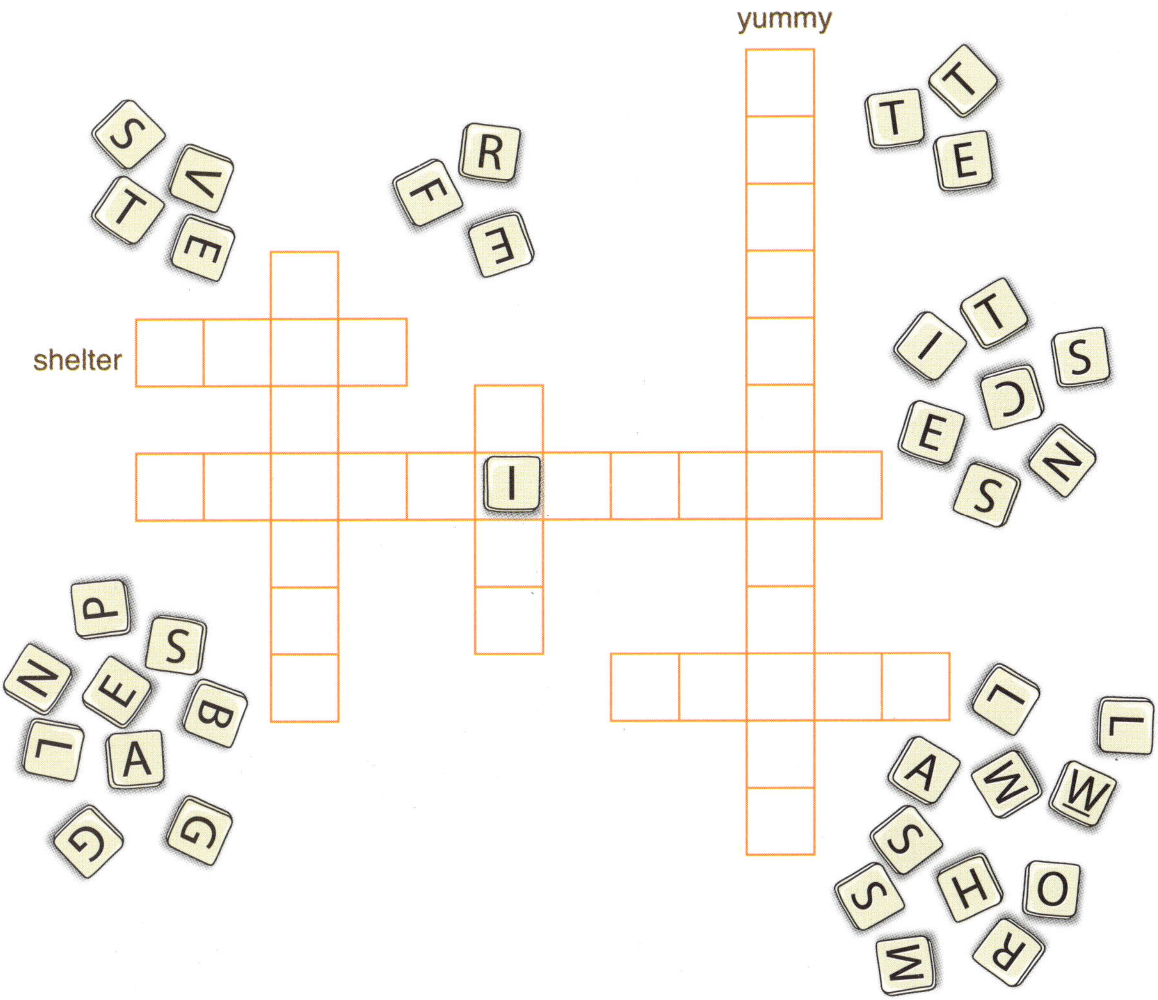

Answer on page 183.

ADD-A-LETTER

Rearrange the tiles from each word, adding one new tile from the bottom in order to form types of heavenly bodies in the empty boxes. Each tile from the bottom of the page is used only once.

R A T

T O M E

V A N

L O R D

P L A T E

R O A S T E D

W C O I N S

Answer on page 184

CROSSED OUT

Use the given tiles to spell a pair of related words that meet on the given letter.

Gecko-pedia

The longest anagram created by a human (Richard Brodie) is a 42,177-word anagram of Jonathan Swift's "Battle of the Books." Of course, a computer can top that: Anagramist Mike Keith used a computer program to generate a 935,763-word anagram of the entire text of "Moby-Dick"!

Answer on page 184.

WORD SWATTER

Use 4 letters from the word below to create 10 common words. Letters will be used more than once but will not repeat in each word.

S A C R E D

				D

A				

	A			

			D	

			E	

D				

				S

		D		

	C			

	E			

Answer on page 184

DROP LETTERS

Use all 3 letter tiles to create 4-letter words below.
Each tile will be used once in per word.

L O S

A			
		G	
			W
			D
		U	
	W		

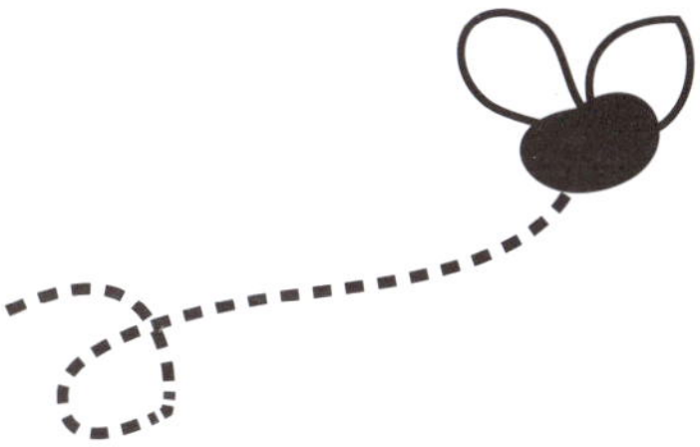

Answer on page 184.

SHUFFLE BOARD

Rearrange each of the letters in the tile groups below to form new words. Place the new words into the grid. One letter has already been placed.

P A R E S   D A D

T H R O W   P O O L

T R E E D

Level

JUMBLED UP

Place each letter into the empty boxes below to create a common word. Tiles are in the correct order, but they are not in the upright position.

J U D G E

Answers on page 184

REPEAT REPEAT

Use the 8 tiles given to complete each pair of words.
Each pair will use the same 4 letter tiles in the same order.

E L N K
H C R A

W		I			L	

	A				D

B	E	A			B			L

				K

Answer on page 184.

CRUNCHED LETTERS

Create 3 words by placing the letter tiles into the grid. Two tiles will be added to the 3-letter sets given—one letter at the beginning and another at the end.

Level

JUMBLED UP

Place each letter into the empty boxes below to create a common word. Tiles are in the correct order, but they are not in the upright position.

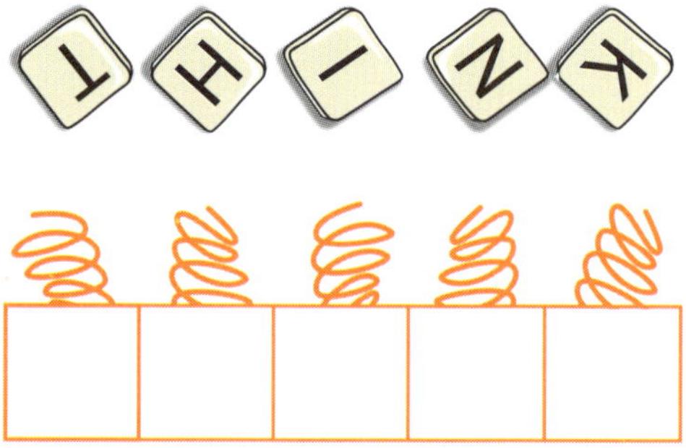

Answers on page 18

THEME PARK

This "ride" has a theme, but we can't tell you what it is. Place all the words in the boxes below—when you do, read the word created in the outlined boxes, from top to bottom, to reveal what the theme is.

CLOCK
CLOSET
DRESSER
LAMP
MIRROR
POSTERS
TABLE

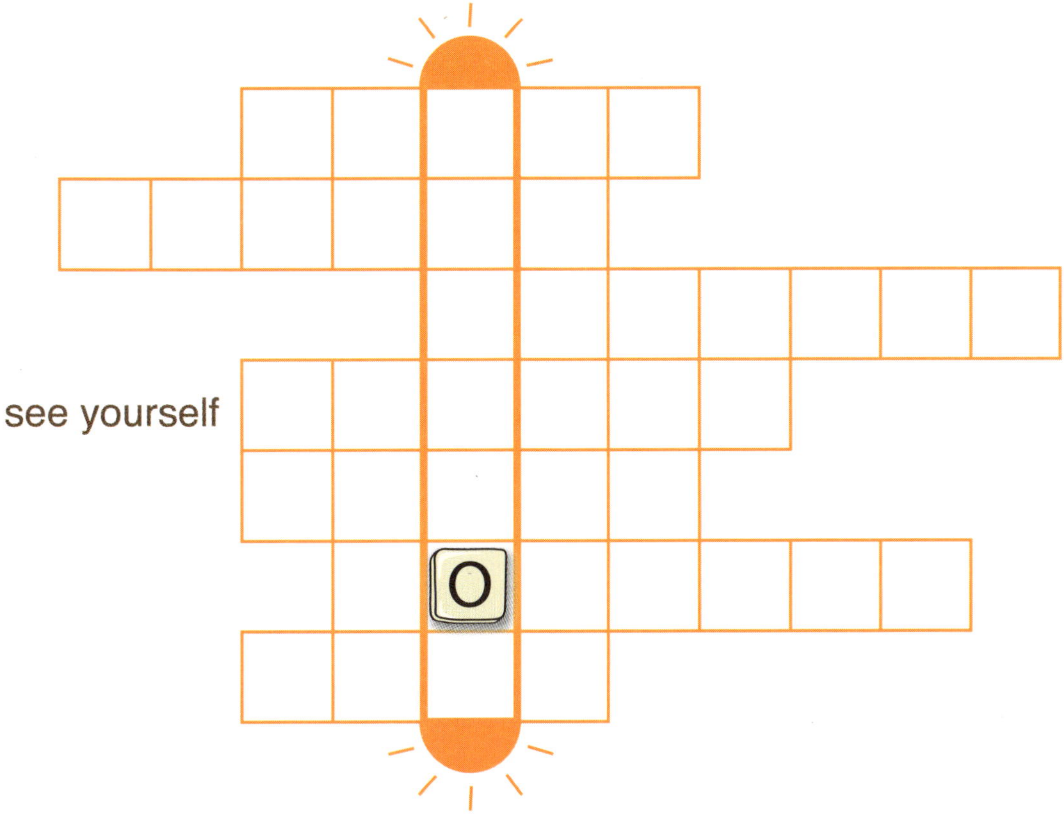

Answer on page 184.

FITTING TILES

In this miniature crossword, the clues are listed randomly. It is up to you to figure out the placement of the 9 answers. To help you, we've inserted 2 letters in the grid, and this is the only occurrence of those letters in the completed puzzle.

CLUES

- Belly button
- Big animals with antlers
- Sound made by touching drinking glasses together
- African country containing Timbuktu
- Stays out of sight
- Tiny part of you that contains your DNA
- Reflection in a mirror
- Measurement that is 1/12 of a foot
- Very enthusiastic

H C I A N E D E L G M I E L N A I S

		V		
				K

Answer on page 18

TILE TIE-INS

Using the letter tiles below, complete the grid to reveal 10 of the months of the year.

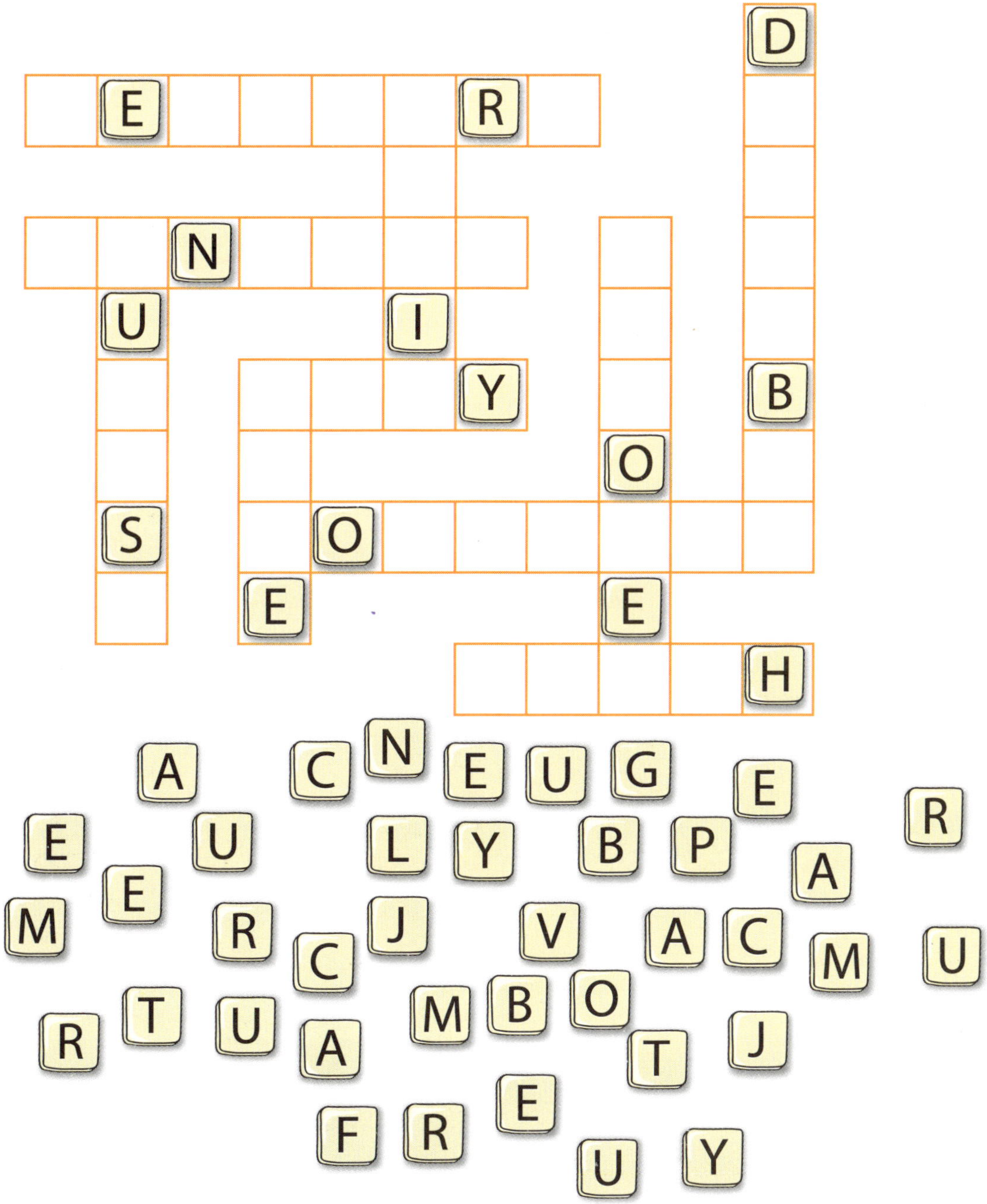

Answer on page 185.

REWORD REWIND

Unscramble the tiles to form words that will complete the sentence.

Our class won a ☐☐☐☐ trip

to see the coral ☐☐☐☐

E R F E

Gecko-pedia

"Retains" has a whopping 13 anagrams! You may recognize many of them, but some of the words are pretty obscure: anestri, asterin, eranist, ratiness, resiant, restain, retinas, retsina, sainter, stainer, starnie, stearin.

Answer on page 18

CROSSED OUT

Use the given tiles to spell a pair of related words that meet on the given letter.

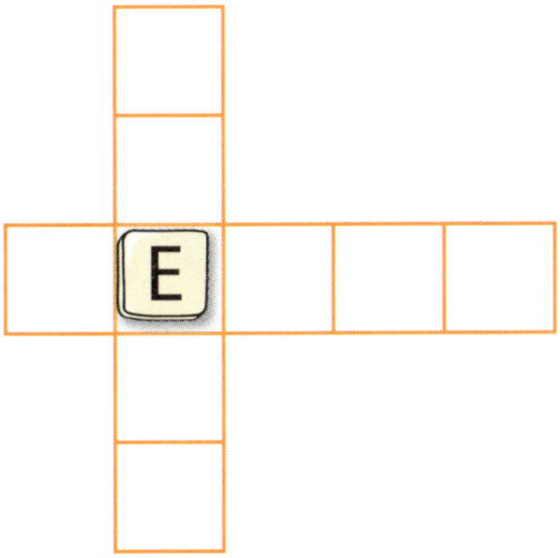

evel

CHAIN WORDS

Place 2 letters in the middle squares that will complete one word and start another. For example, ER would complete FLI – ER– ORR.

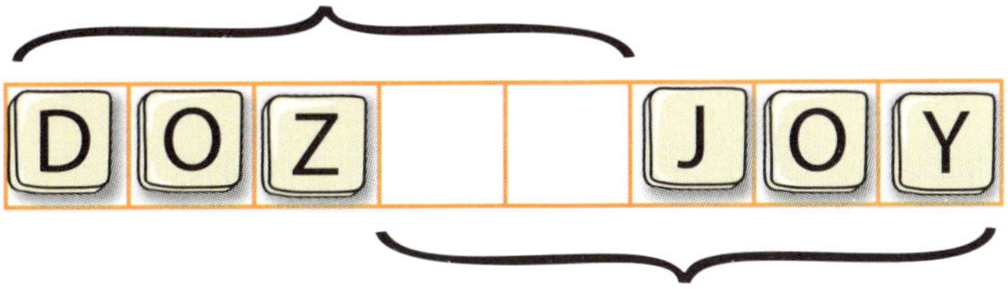

Answers on page 185.

ALPHABET EXPRESS

Use every letter tile below to complete the grid with common words.

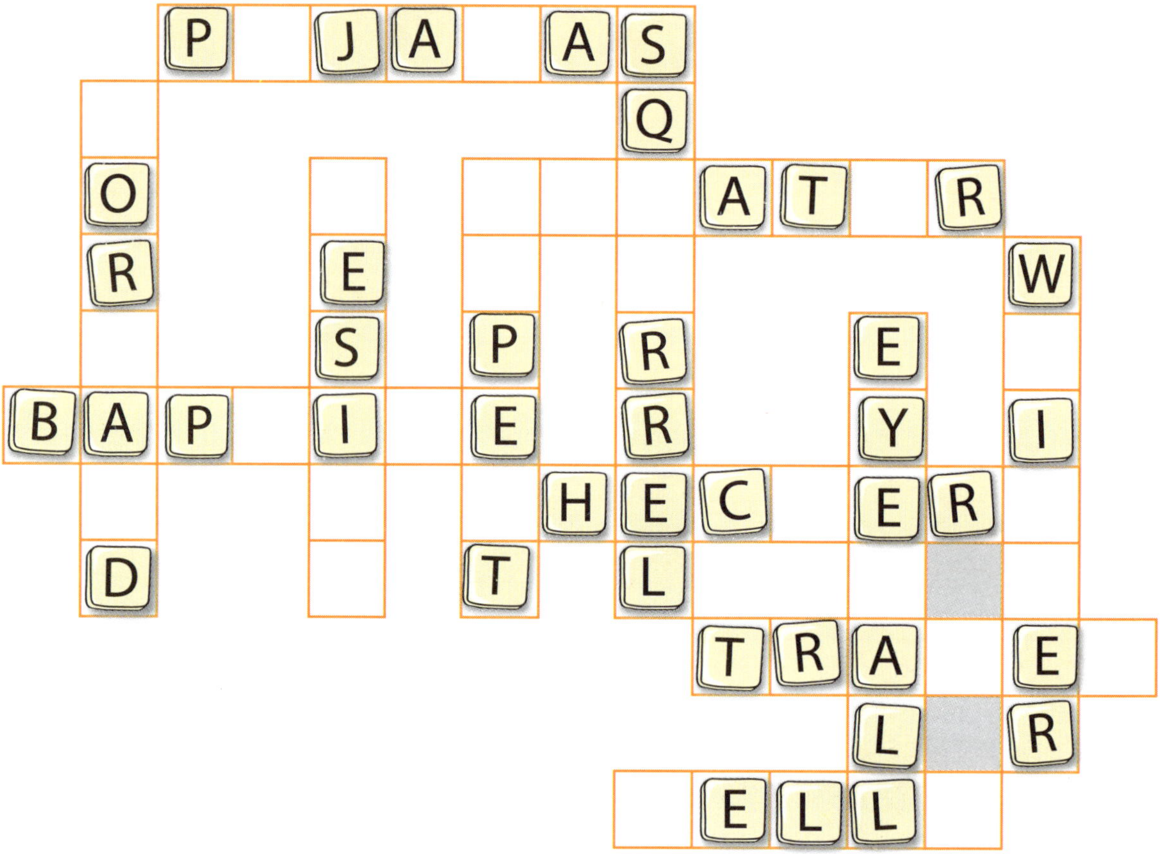

A B C D E F G H I

J K L M N O P Q

R S T U V W X Y Z

Answer on page 185

ONE UP

Use the 3 tiles at the bottom of the page to solve the bottom clue. Once you do that, move up the page, solving each clue as you go. Carry all the letters used from one clue to the next, rearranging them in the empty spaces.

_ _ _ E _ _ _ _ _ ····· Observe a holiday

B _ _ _ _ _ _ _ ····· Wrist jewelry

T _ _ _ _ _ _ ····· Molasses candy

_ E _ _ _ _ ····· Breakfast food

_ _ _ _ R ····· Free from obstructions

L _ _ _ ····· Delicate fabric

_ _ _ ····· High card

C A E

Answer on page 185.

PLUS ONE

Using the letters in the top 3 tiles, create 3 new 4-letter words by adding one of the letters from the bottom 3 tiles.

H E M

P L T

L A D

O Y G

Answer on page 185

DROP LETTERS

Use all 3 letter tiles to create 4-letter words below.
Each tile will be used once per word.

L G U

			F
P			
			Y
			E
		N	
			P

Answer on page 185.

COME TOGETHER

Place each of the tile sets into the empty spaces below to create 3 nine-letter U.S. states. Each tile set is used only once.

LOU NES SEY

MIN JER ANA

NEW ISI OTA

Answer on page 185

PILES O' TILES

Place all the tiles into the grid so they spell things you might find at a birthday party. The tiles are compiled in specific groups—those groups will appear together in across or down entries.

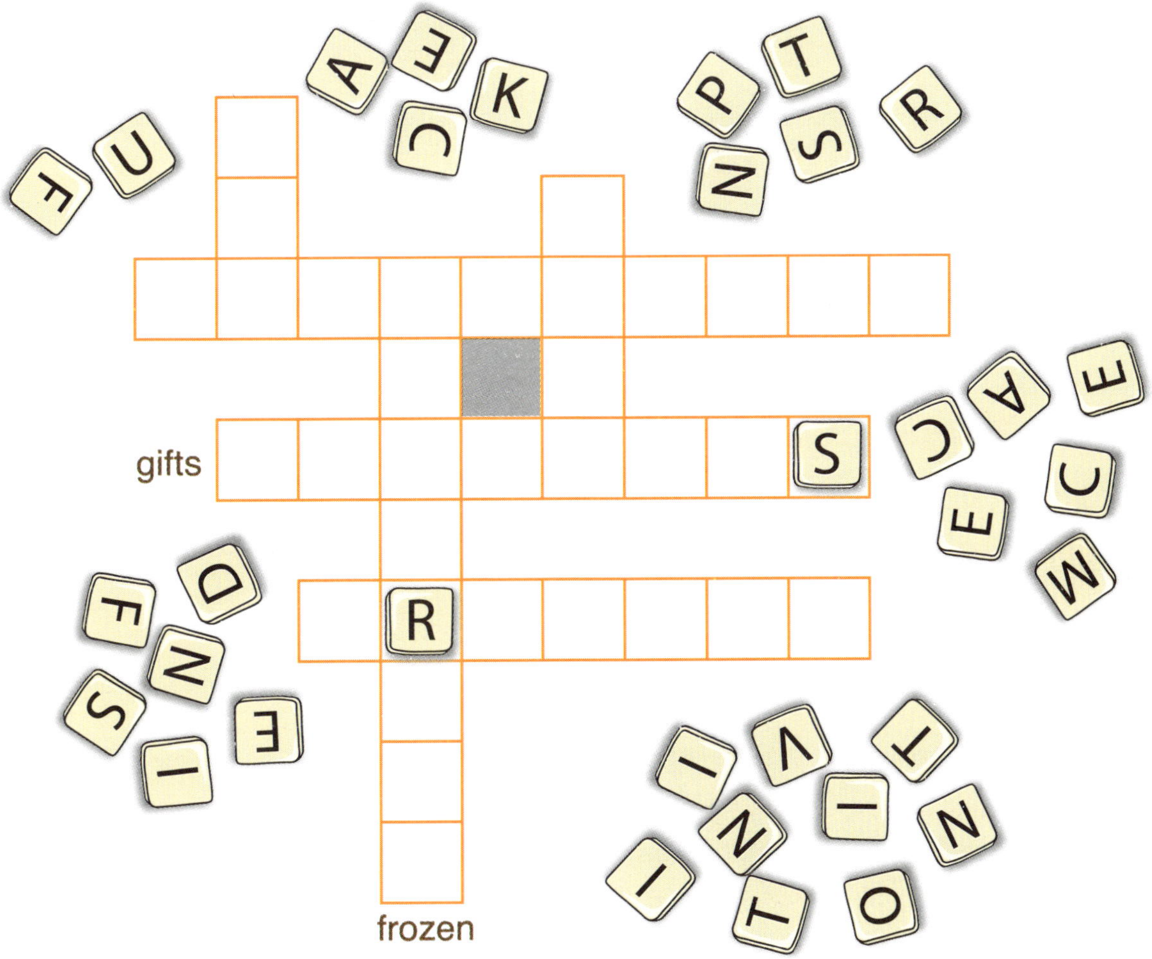

Answer on page 186.

WORD STICKERS

Use the letter tiles given to complete the word pairs. Each pair of words will be a synonym (words with similar meanings) of one another.

E T N S
T E O A

B				

M			S			R

R E R T
A E S A

	P			

	X			

Answer on page 186

TILE TIE-INS

Using the letter tiles below, complete the grid to reveal 12 world capitals.

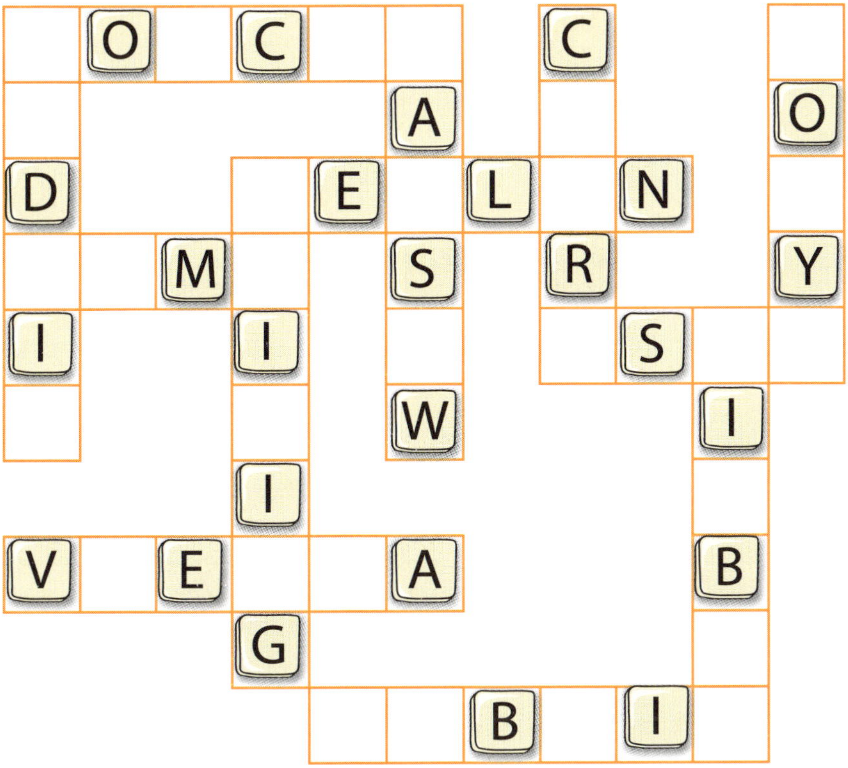

Answer on page 186.

ADD-A-LETTER

Rearrange the tiles from each word, adding one new tile from the bottom in order to form an article of clothing in the empty boxes. Each tile from the bottom of the page is used only once.

R E D S

K I T S

T A P S

C A R S

W A T E R S

S A N E

S L A W

F E J H N R S

Answer on page 18

THEME PARK

This "ride" has a theme, but we can't tell you what it is. Place all the words in the boxes below—when you do, read the word created in the outlined boxes, from top to bottom, to reveal what the theme is.

BOTTLE	DIAPER
BURP	NURSE
CRIES	SPIT UP

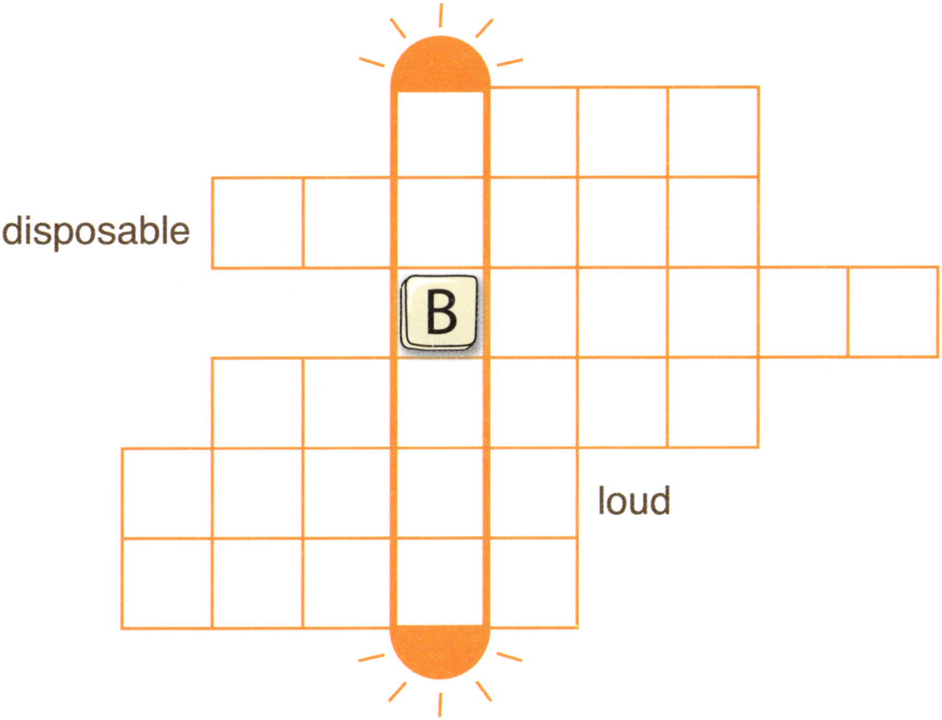

Answer on page 186.

FITTING TILES

In this miniature crossword, the clues are listed randomly. It is up to you to figure out the placement of the 9 answers. To help you, we've inserted 2 letters in the grid, and this is the only occurrence of those letters in the completed puzzle.

CLUES

- People older than 12 but younger than 20
- "Keep quiet!"
- Abandon
- Wedding cake layer
- Our planet
- July 4, 1776, is an example of one
- "Goodbye," in French
- Penny coin
- Bright thought

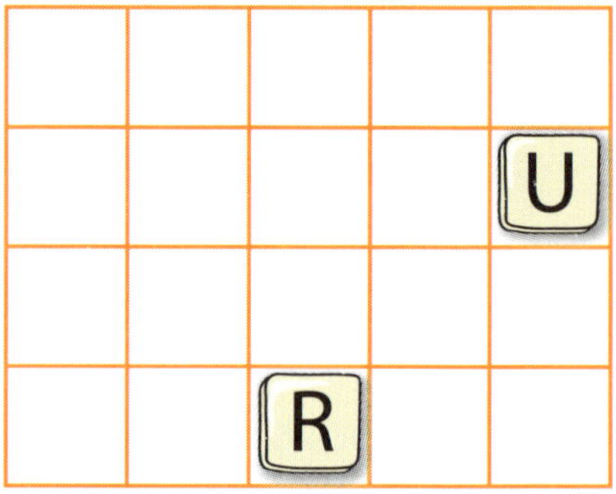

Answer on page 18

CRUNCHED LETTERS

Create 3 words by placing the letter tiles into the grid. Two tiles will be added to the 3-letter sets given—one letter at the beginning and another at the end.

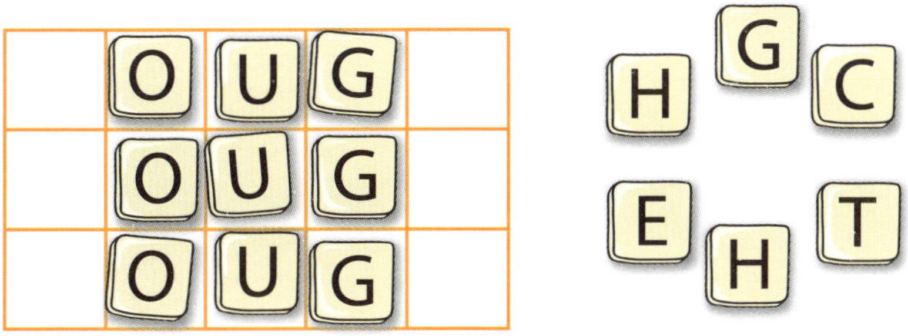

evel

JUMBLED UP

Place each letter into the empty boxes below to create a common word. Tiles are in the correct order, but they are not in the upright position.

Answers on page 186.

LETTER GRIDLOCK

Use the given tiles to complete the grid with words reading across and down. Use the clues, which are assorted randomly, to help discover the missing words.

CLUES

- Arm joint
- Strange
- Distress signal letters
- Gets better
- Head warmer
- Letters are put in here
- Misfortune
- Moisture on the grass
- Some soccer players
- Sets of 3

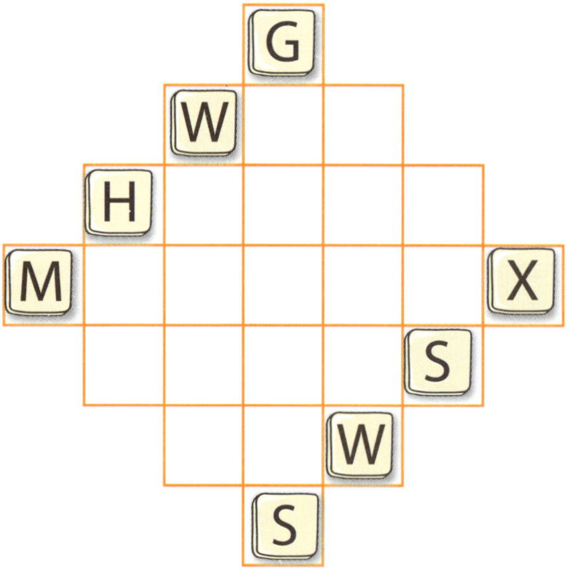

Answer on page 18

CROSSED OUT

Use the given tiles to spell a pair of related words that meet on the given letter.

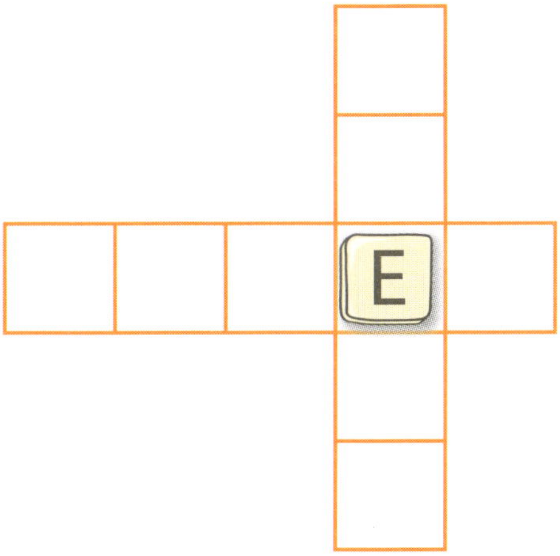

Gecko-pedia

A panagram is a sentence that uses every letter of the alphabet at least once. Here's an example: Watch "Jeopardy!," Alex Trebek's fun TV quiz game.

Answer on page 186.

DROP LETTERS

Use all 3 letter tiles to create 4-letter words below.
Each tile will be used once per word.

W D E

	I		
O			
		L	
	R		
A			
			Y

Answer on page 187

PLUS ONE

Using the letters in the top 3 tiles, create 3 new 4-letter words by adding one of the letters from the bottom 3 tiles.

A N T	W A N
☐☐☐☐	☐☐☐☐
☐☐☐☐	☐☐☐☐
☐☐☐☐	☐☐☐☐
E U W	R D S

Answer on page 187.

REPEAT REPEAT

Use the 8 tiles given to complete each pair of words.
Each pair will use the same 4 letter tiles in the same order.

P N I L

E R S A

	R	E	M				E

S			D			S

A		I	M			

S			I		

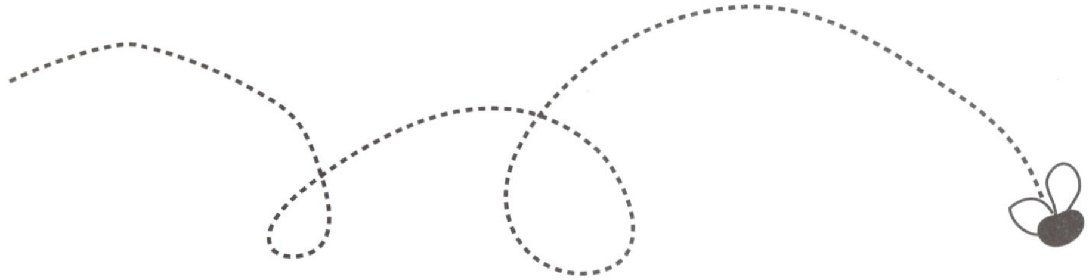

Answer on page 187

REWORD REWIND

Unscramble the tiles to form words that will complete the sentence.

The chef took a road trip to [ ][ ][ ][ ][ ]

a bowl of soup from every U.S. [ ][ ][ ][ ][ ]

T T A E S

evel

CHAIN WORDS

Place 3 letters in the middle squares that will complete one word and start another. For example, TAR would complete GUI – TAR – GET.

G L O [ ][ ][ ] L E T

Answers on page 187.

ONE UP

Use the 3 tiles at the bottom of the page to solve the bottom clue. Once you do that, move up the page, solving each clue as you go. Carry all the letters used from one clue to the next, rearranging them in the empty spaces.

_ _ _ H _ _ _ _ _ ······ Bad dream

_ _ I _ _ _ _ _ ······ Someone who moves to another country

_ _ R _ _ _ _ ······ Piece of clothing

M _ _ _ _ _ ······ Object that attracts iron

_ _ _ N _ ······ Artist's representative

_ _ T _ ······ Opening in a fence

_ _ _ ······ Birthday number

E G A

Answer on page 187

COME TOGETHER

Place each of the tile sets into the empty spaces below to create 3 nine-letter birds. Each tile set is used only once.

RED REN BAR

OWL AWK SEW

HOU HTH NIG

Answer on page 187.

WORD SWATTER

Use 5 letters from the word below to create 6 common words. Letters will be used more than once but will not repeat in each word.

S E A T B E L T

		B		

	T			

				T

		T		

	E			

	A			

Gecko-pedia

Ever switch the letters around in a sentence? Then you've stumbled into a spoonerism! Named after Reverend William Arthur Spooner, spoonerisms are when you unintentionally swap sounds to wake new mords. Er... that's make new words!

Answer on page 187

ALPHABET EXPRESS

Use every letter tile below to complete the grid with common words.

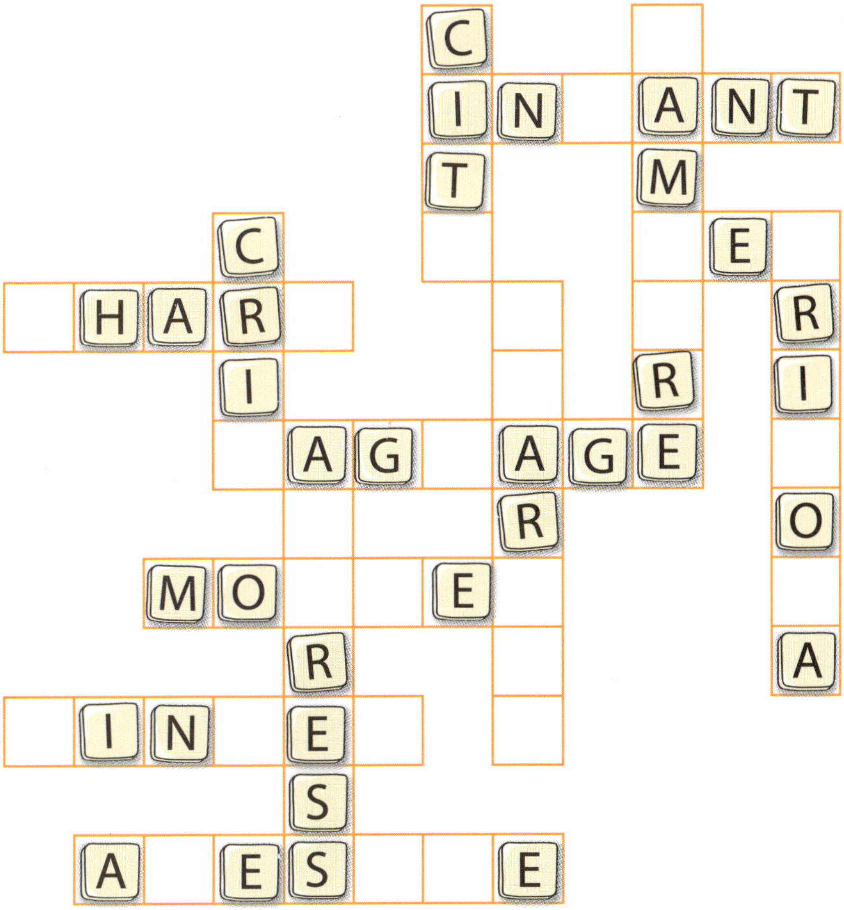

A B C D E F G H I

J K L M N O P Q

R S T U V W X Y Z

Answer on page 188.

THEME PARK

This "ride" has a theme, but we can't tell you what it is. Place all the words in the boxes below—when you do, read the word created in the outlined boxes, from top to bottom, to reveal what the theme is.

APRIL FOOL'S	FLAG	MOTHER'S
BIRTH	GROUNDHOG	ST. PATRICK'S
CINCO DE MAYO	IDES OF MARCH	VALENTINE'S
FATHER'S	MAY	

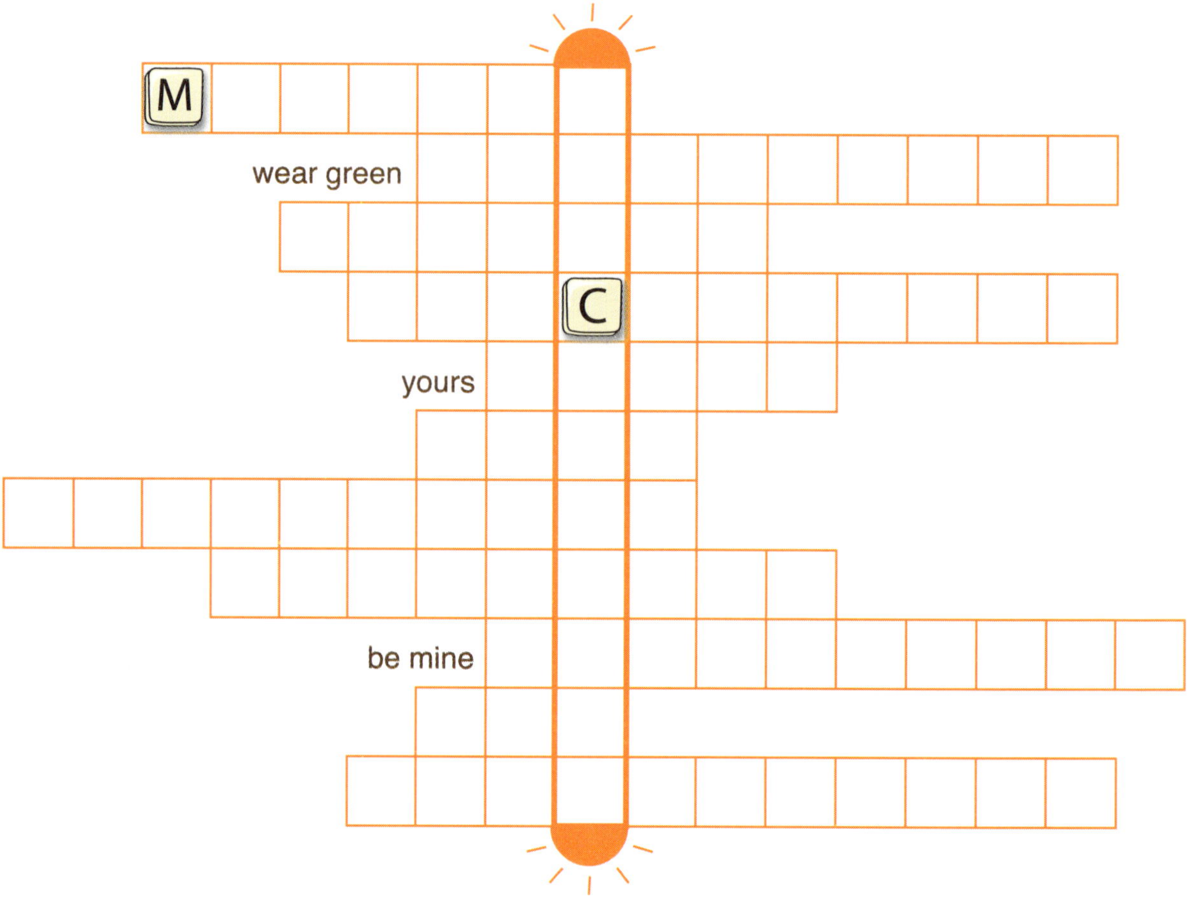

Answer on page 18

FITTING TILES

In this miniature crossword, the clues are listed randomly. It is up to you to figure out the placement of the 9 answers. To help you, we've inserted 2 letters in the grid, and this is the only occurrence of those letters in the completed puzzle.

CLUES

- Not under
- Halloween costume that uses a white sheet
- Superman, for example
- Not even once
- Talking on and on
- Flat item used for carrying food in a cafeteria
- Sports stadium
- E-mail button
- Chew on something tough

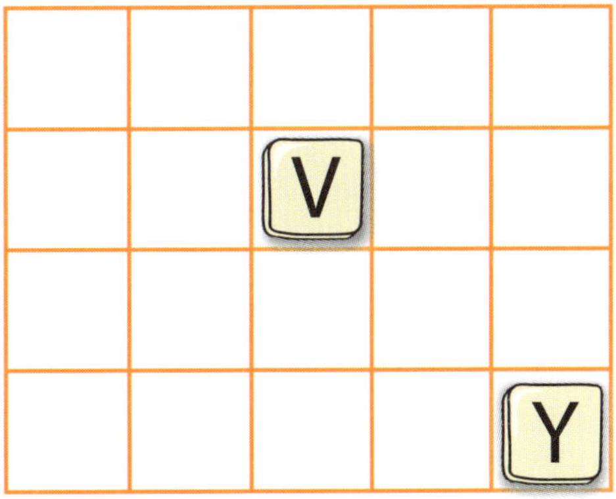

Answer on page 188.

TILE TIE-INS

Using the letter tiles below, complete the grid to reveal 9 types of ice cream toppings.

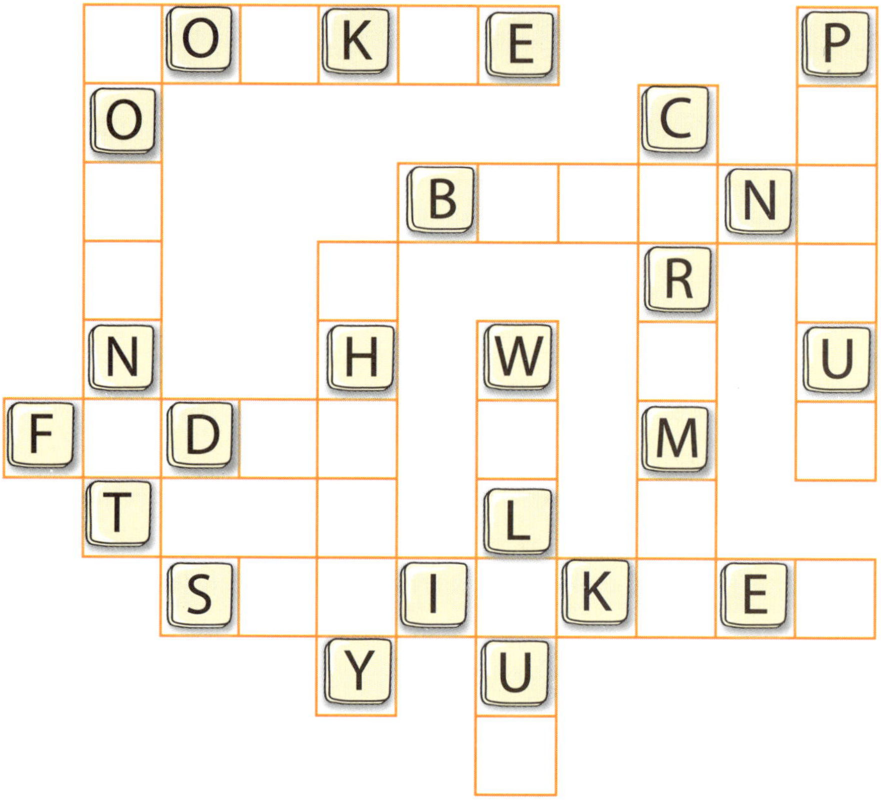

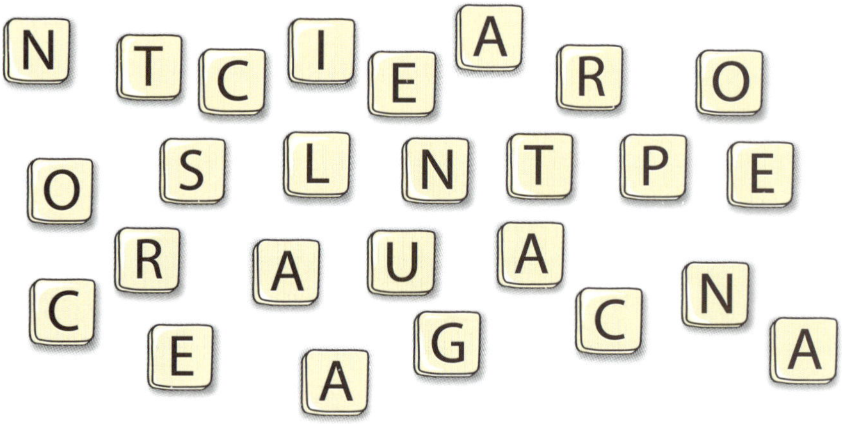

Answer on page 18

CRUNCHED LETTERS

Create 3 words by placing the letter tiles into the grid. Two tiles will be added to the 3-letter sets given—one letter at the beginning and another at the end.

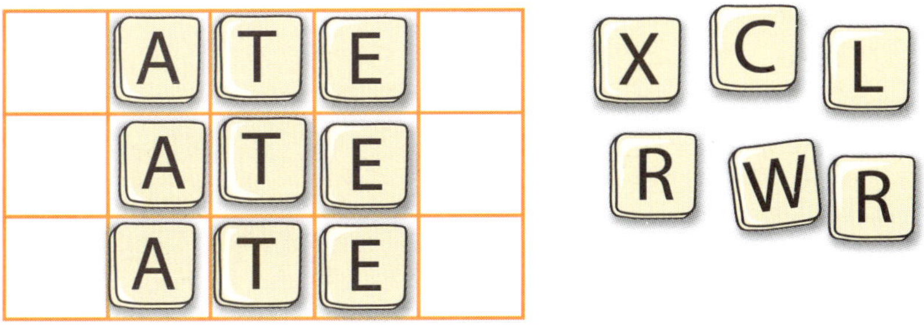

evel

JUMBLED UP

Place each letter into the empty boxes below to create a common word. Tiles are in the correct order, but they are not in the upright position.

Answers on page 188.

PILES O' TILES

Place all the tiles into the grid so they spell the names of some truly super heroes. The tiles are compiled in specific groups—those groups will appear together in across or down entries.

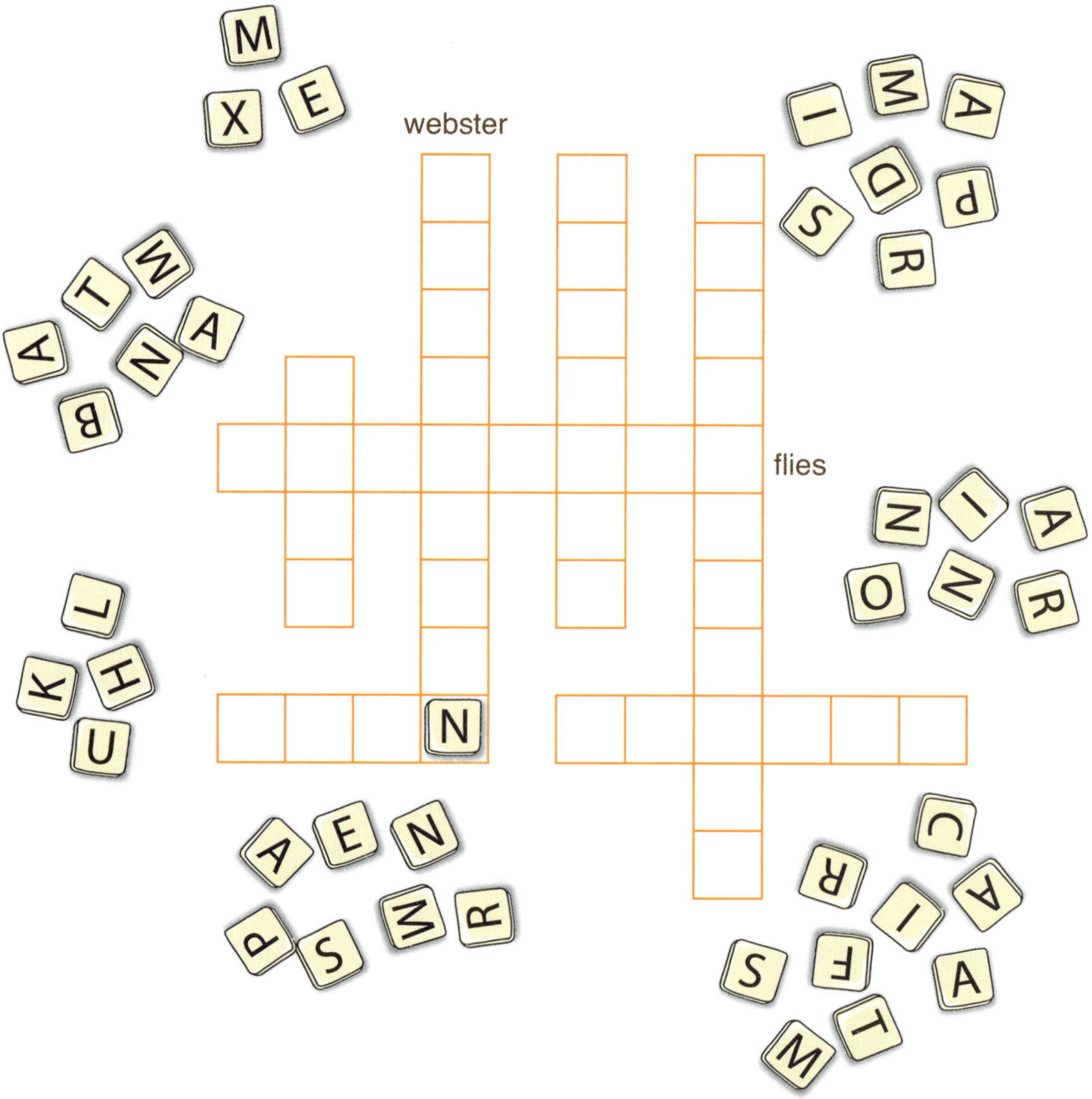

Answer on page 18

SHUFFLE BOARD

Rearrange each of the letters in the words below to form new words. Place the new words into the grid. One letter has already been placed.

P A C E S   S P A R E

P R A T E   S T R A P

S U E

Gecko-pedia

Estimates range from 250,000 to 750,000, but there is no real way to know just how many words are in the English language. What's great about our language is that it's always growing—the "Oxford English Dictionary" adds about 10,000 words and phrases every year!

Answer on page 189.

ADD-A-LETTER

Rearrange the tiles from each word, adding one new tile from the bottom in order to form a type of cheese in the empty boxes. Each tile from the bottom of the page is used only once.

C R I B ☐☐☐☐☐

M A R E ☐☐☐☐☐

M A D ☐☐☐☐

T A G ☐☐☐☐

A T E ☐☐☐☐

A R C H E D ☐☐☐☐☐☐☐

G O A D ☐☐☐☐☐

U O E D F K C

Answer on page 18

REPEAT REPEAT

Use the 8 tiles given to complete each pair of words.
Each pair will use the same 4 letter tiles in the same order.

H S F N
O E R C

			R	I	F	

			L	

M	A		A				I

			W		S

Answer on page 189.

WORD STICKERS

Use the letter tiles given to complete the word pairs. Each pair of words will be a homonym (words that sound alike, but are spelled differently) of one another.

E W L

L B B

		E	
		U	

R E A

S E R

C		L	L		
		L	L	E	

Answer on page 18

LETTER GRIDLOCK

Use the given tiles to complete the grid with words reading across and down. Use the clues, which are assorted randomly, to help discover the missing words.

CLUES

- "___ Goes the Weasel"
- A note to follow fa
- Drinking tube
- Fuel for a car
- Like a house full of ghosts
- Part of a bloom
- Pull thread with a needle
- Sticks out the bottom lip
- Tight braid of hair
- Wounds with a tusk

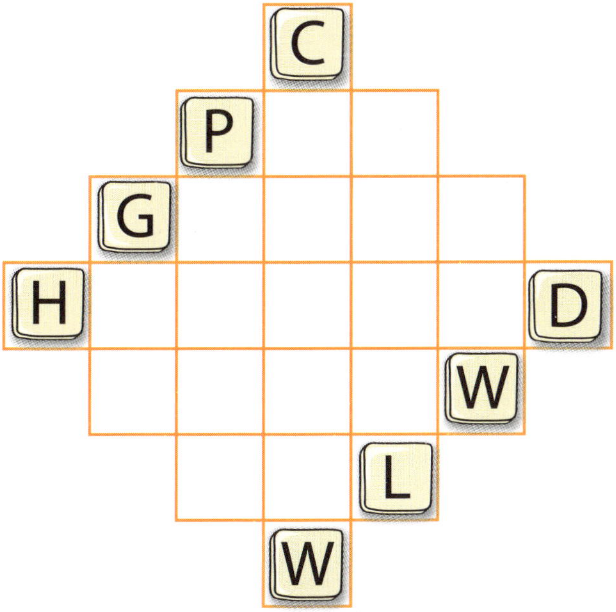

Answer on page 189.

COME TOGETHER

Place each of the tile sets into the empty spaces below to create 3 nine-letter birds. Each tile set is used only once.

C K B   N C H   G O L

D F I   G L E   B L A

D E A   I R D   B A L

Answer on page 18

JUMBLED UP

Place each letter into the empty boxes below to create a common word. Tiles are in the correct order, but they are not in the upright position.

Gecko-pedia

A palindrome is a word or phrase that can be read the same either forward or backward. "Nun" is one example, "deed" is another. Some palindromes run much, much longer than that. In fact, French writer Georges Perec created a palindrome that was 5,556 letters long!

Answer on page 189.

REPEAT REPEAT

Use the 8 tiles given to complete each pair of words.
Each pair will use the same 4 letter tiles in the same order.

N C R O
F D E I

K		T		H		
T	H			K		

	L			I		A

			C	E	

Answer on page 18

ONE UP

Use the 3 tiles at the bottom of the page to solve the bottom clue. Once you do that, move up the page, solving each clue as you go. Carry all the letters used from one clue to the next, rearranging them in the empty spaces.

B _ _ _ _ _ _ _ _	Swimming stroke
F _ _ _ _ _ _ _	Flapping in the breeze
_ _ _ _ _ _ Y	Completely
_ _ _ _ L _	Slow-moving reptile
_ T _ _ _	Put into words
_ _ _ E	Loyal
_ _ _	Cart track

U R T

Answer on page 189.

WORD SWATTER

Use 3 letters from the words below to create 3 common words. Letters will be used more than once but will not repeat in each word.

S T O P   I N

P	O			
	I			S
		N	T	

Doing puzzles gives you mental exercise, which is just as important as physical exercise!

Gecko-pedia

The word puzzle "Jumble" was first created in 1954 by a comic book artist—if he were a comic book superhero, you might call him Jumble Man!

Answer on page 19C

THEME PARK

This "ride" has a theme, but we can't tell you what it is. Place all the words in the boxes below—when you do, read the word created in the outlined boxes, from top to bottom, to reveal what the theme is.

AUSTRALIA	ENGLAND	MEXICO
CANADA	ITALY	RUSSIA
CHINA	KOREA	USA

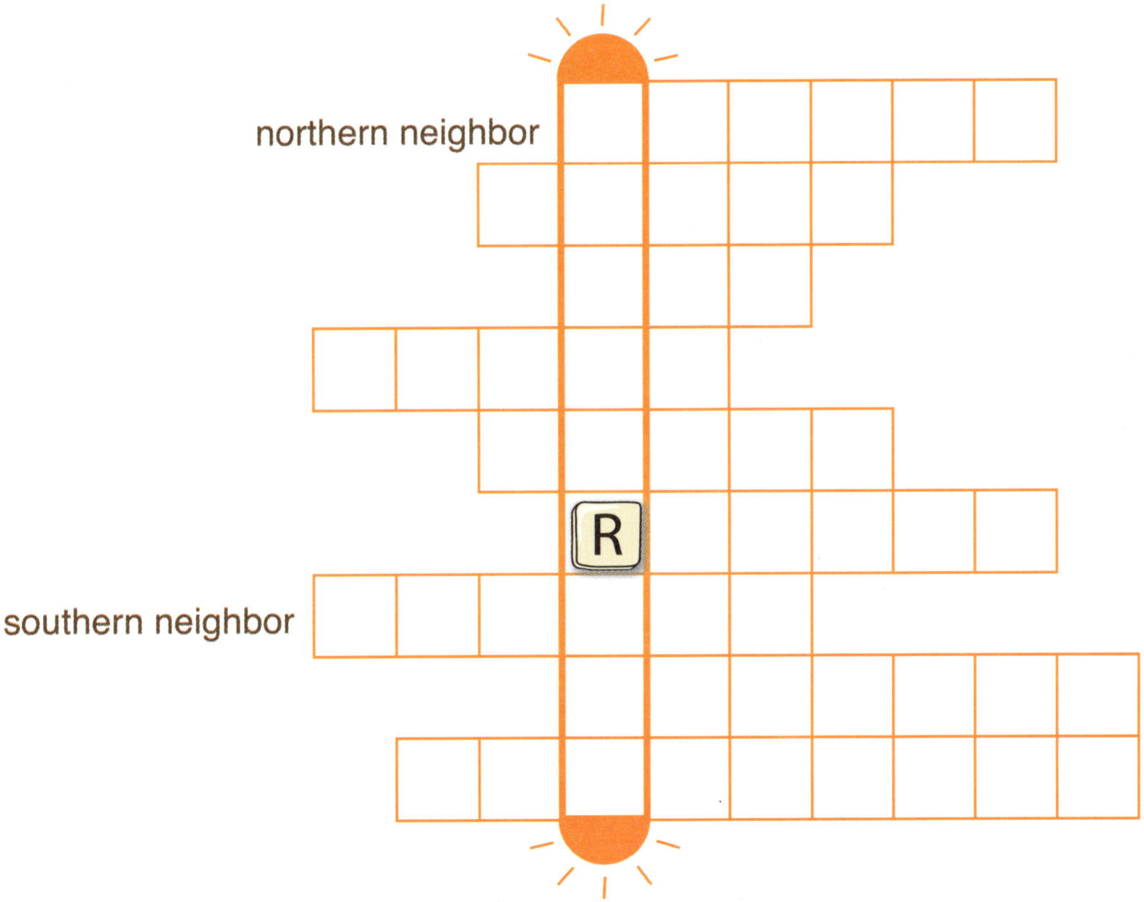

Answer on page 190.

TILE TIE-INS

Using the letter tiles below, complete the grid to reveal 9 familiar shapes.

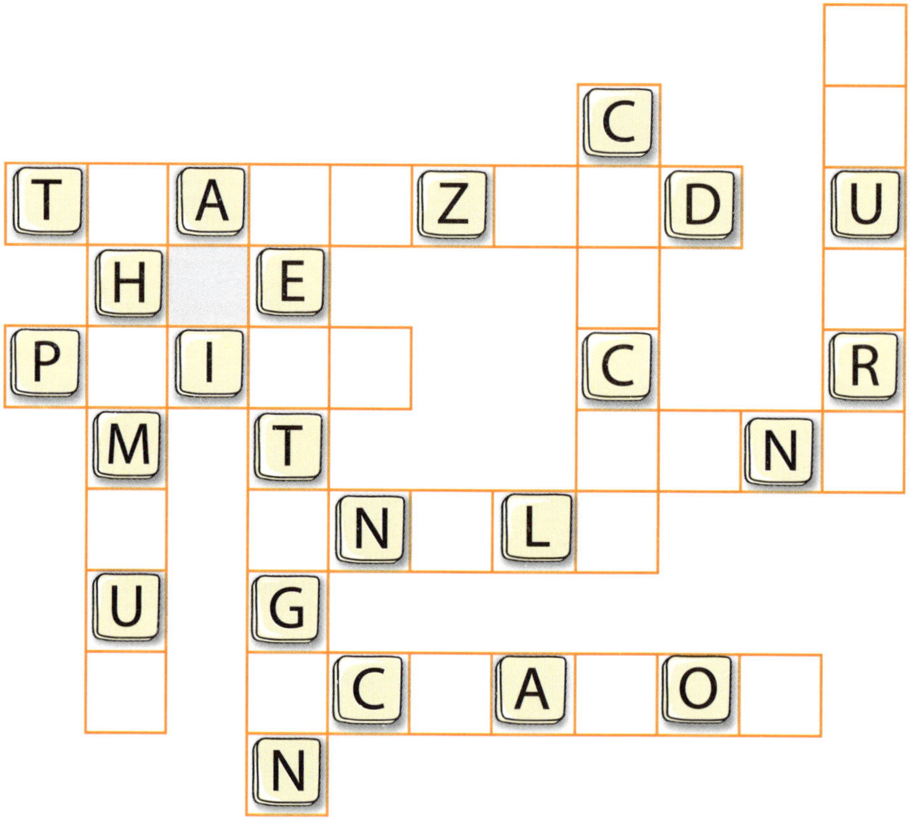

Answer on page 190

FITTING TILES

In this miniature crossword, the clues are listed randomly. It is up to you to figure out the placement of the 9 answers. To help you, we've inserted 2 letters in the grid, and this is the only occurrence of those letters in the completed puzzle.

CLUES

- Colored part of your eye
- An archer shoots it at a target
- Job for a detective
- Not moving at all
- ____ and crafts
- These letters: S S S S S
- Wise birds
- Capital of Egypt
- Actor's part in a play

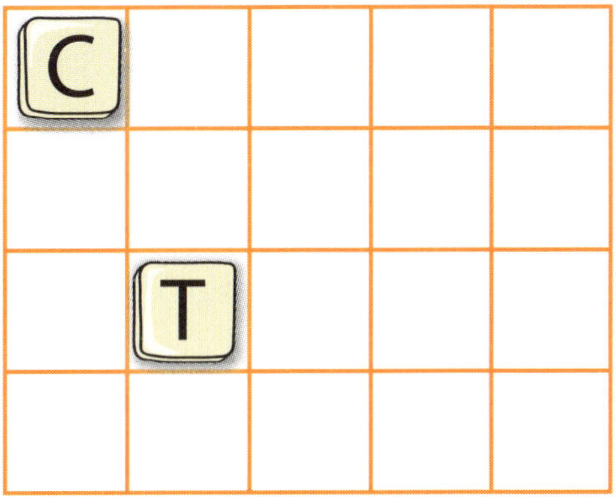

Answer on page 190.

CHAIN WORDS

Place 2 letters in the middle squares that will complete one word and start another. For example, ER would complete FLI – ER – ROR.

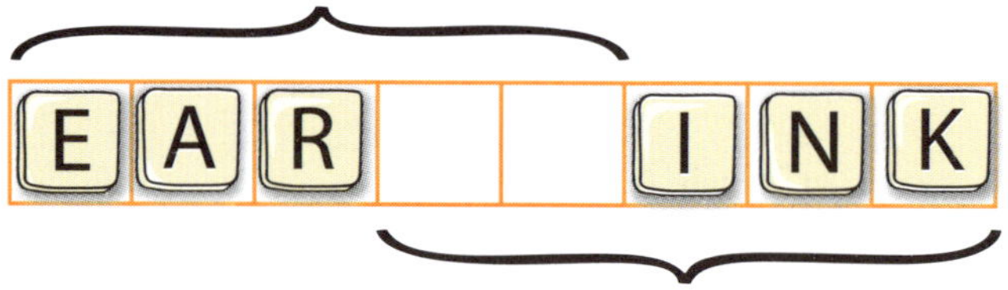

Level

CROSSED OUT

Use the given tiles to spell a pair of related words that meet on the given letter.

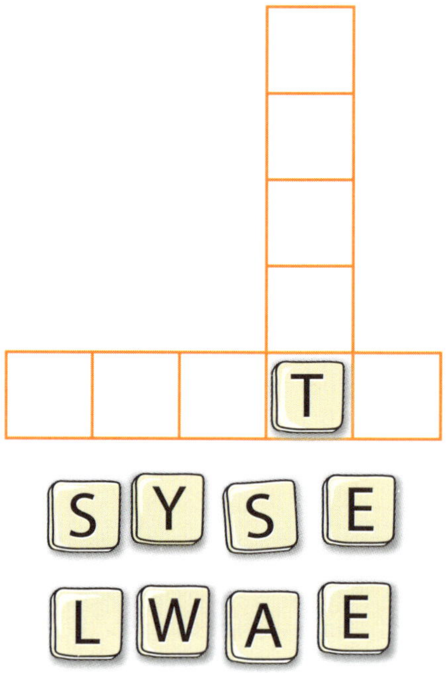

Answers on page 190

PLUS ONE

Using the letters in the top 3 tiles, create 3 new 4-letter words by adding one of the letters from the bottom 3 tiles.

F A R

A I M

H U G

S E N

Answer on page 190.

CRUNCHED LETTERS

Create 3 words by placing the letters tiles into the grid. Two tiles will be added to the 3-letter sets given—one letter at the beginning and another at the end.

	O	N	E	
	O	N	E	
	O	N	E	

S H R

Y L B

Gecko-pedia

Who doesn't love to laugh? We've got all sorts of words for laughter, some more obscure than others. Kench, for instance, means to "laugh loudly." Nicker? "A neighing laugh." And snirt? "To snicker!"

Answer on page 190

REWORD REWIND

Unscramble the tiles to form words that will complete the sentence.

The farmer loved Raisin [ ][ ][ ][ ] so much,

he kept a box in his red [ ][ ][ ][ ]

R A N B

WORD STICKERS

Use the letter tiles given to complete the word pairs. Each pair of words will be a synonym (words with similar meanings) of one another.

E T I

T E U U

Q [ ][ ][ ][ ]

M [ ][ ][ ] D

I E Y

E L E T

S [ ][ ][ ] P [ ]

[ ][ ] R [ ] D

Answers on page 190.

ADD-A-LETTER

Rearrange the tiles from each word, adding one new tile from the bottom in order to form a type of transportation in the empty boxes. Each tile from the bottom of the page is used only once.

O U T	☐ ☐ ☐ ☐
O I L	☐ ☐ ☐ ☐
T A B	☐ ☐ ☐ ☐
D E A N	☐ ☐ ☐ ☐ ☐
H I S	☐ ☐ ☐ ☐
I R A N	☐ ☐ ☐ ☐ ☐

O M T S P A

Answer on page 19

COME TOGETHER

Place each of the tile sets into the empty spaces below to create 3 nine-letter birds. Each tile set is used only once.

D P I	D G E	B L A
P E R	C K T	S A N
T R I	E R N	P A R

Answer on page 191.

ALPHABET EXPRESS

Use every letter tile below to complete the grid with common words.

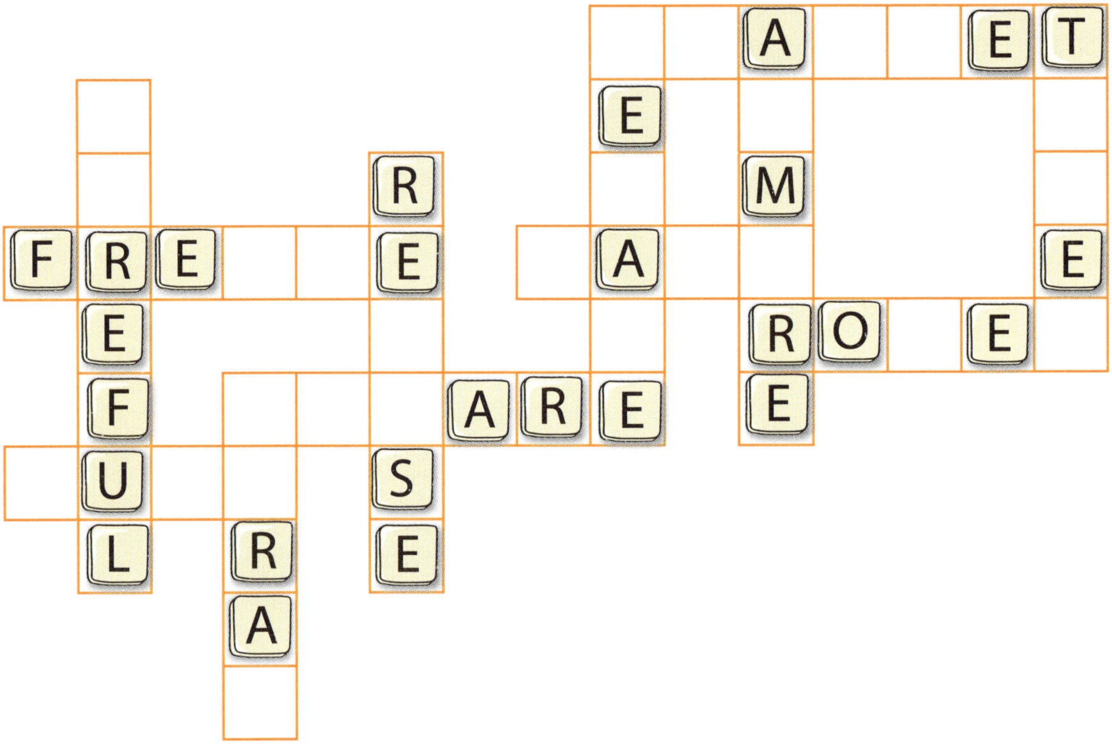

C F J K X Y P L Q

Z B R I U M H T E

D O A N S W V G

Answer on page 19

DROP LETTERS

Use all 3 letter tiles to create 4-letter words below.
Each tile will be used once per word.

C I N

			H
	O		
		O	
			E
	H		
Z			

Answer on page 191.

LETTER GRIDLOCK

Use the given tiles to complete the grid with words reading across and down. Use the clues, which are assorted randomly, to help discover the missing words.

CLUES

- Where to wear a watch
- Use your eyes
- Use the oars
- Scoffs
- Polished part of a foot
- Plane without propellers
- Make fun of
- Humor
- Copper coins
- Continue a subscription

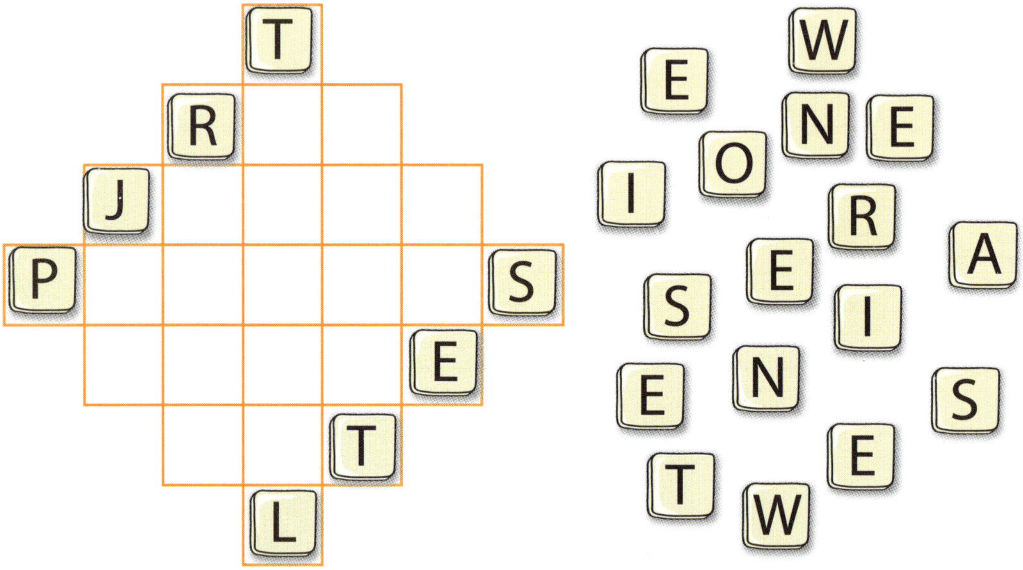

Answer on page 19

SHUFFLE BOARD

Rearrange each of the letters in the words below to form new words. Place the new words into the grid. One letter has already been placed.

C H E A P   P A I N S

M A R   P E E L S

T H O R N

N				

Answer on page 191.

JUMBLED UP

Place each letter into the empty boxes below to create a common word. Tiles are in the correct order, but they are not in the upright position.

Level

CROSSED OUT

Use the given tiles to spell a pair of related words that meet on the given letter.

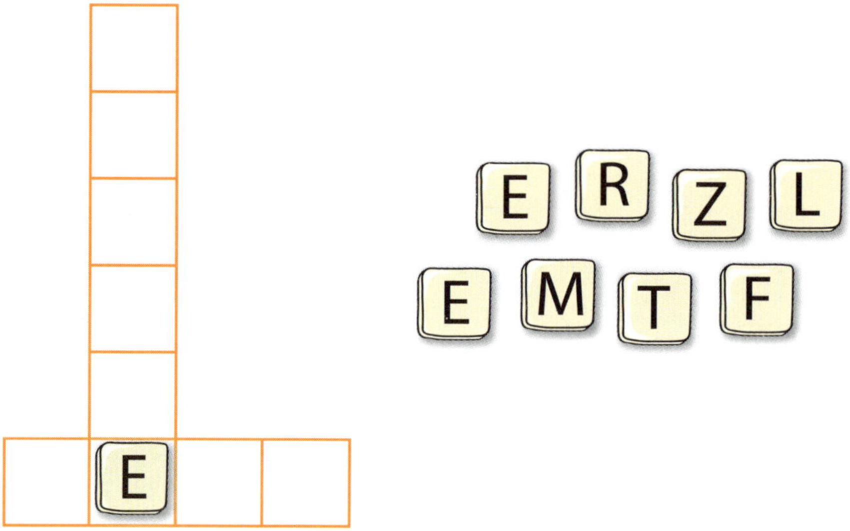

Answers on page 19

ALPHABET EXPRESS

Use every letter tile below to complete the grid with common words.

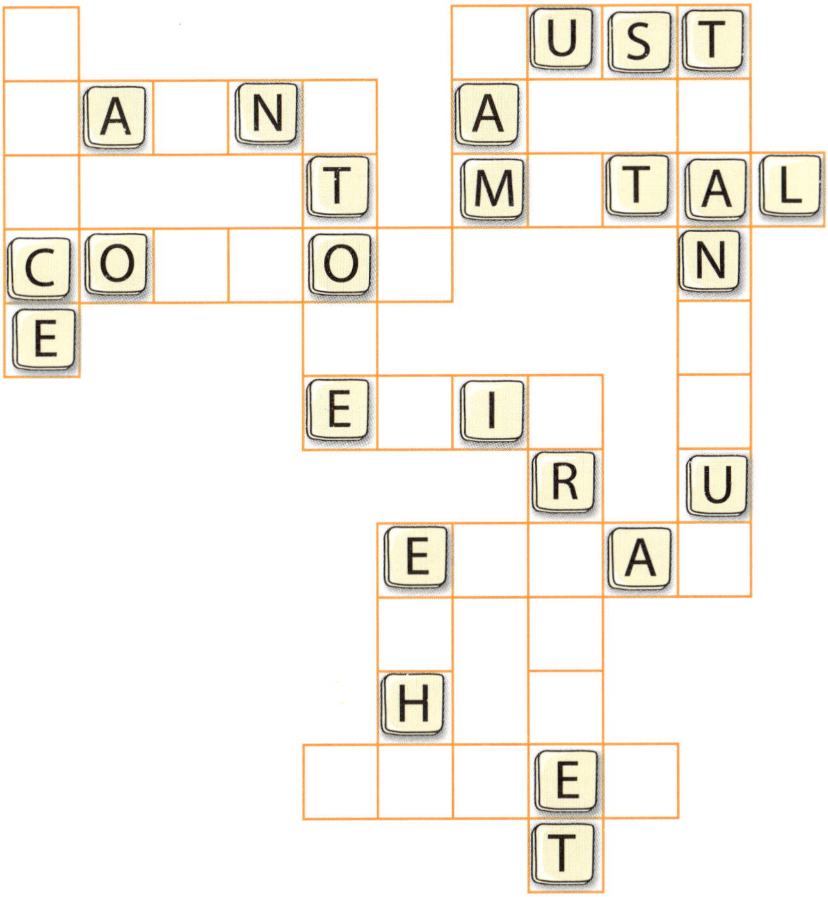

Answer on page 191.

THEME PARK

This "ride" has a theme, but we can't tell you what it is. Place all the words in the boxes below—when you do, read the word created in the outlined boxes, from top to bottom, to reveal what the theme is.

CLARINET	HORN	TRUMPET
CYMBALS	OBOE	TUBA
DRUM	SAXOPHONE	VIOLIN
FLUTE	TROMBONE	

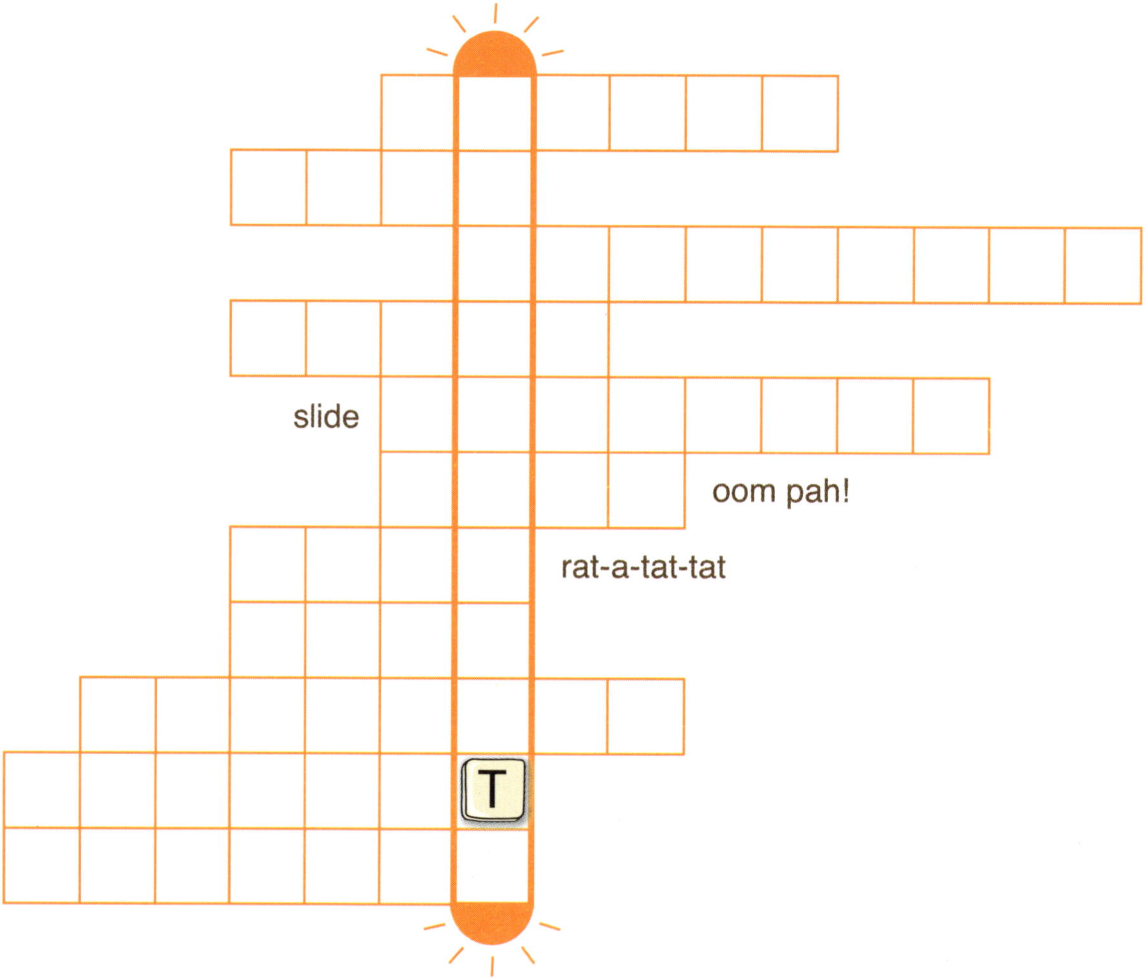

Answer on page 192

One Up (page 6)

STREAMERS
ARMRESTS
SMARTER
MASTER
STEAM
STEM
MET

Add-a-Letter (page 7)

LION
TIGER
BEAR
LLAMA
CAMEL
BISON

Reword Rewind (page 8)

spear/pears

Chain Words (page 8)

VACANTHEM

Alphabet Express (page 9)

Word Swatter (page 10)

Answers may vary.

LIED LIKE
IDLE LEND
KIND DINE
LINK DELI

Tile Tie-Ins (page 11)

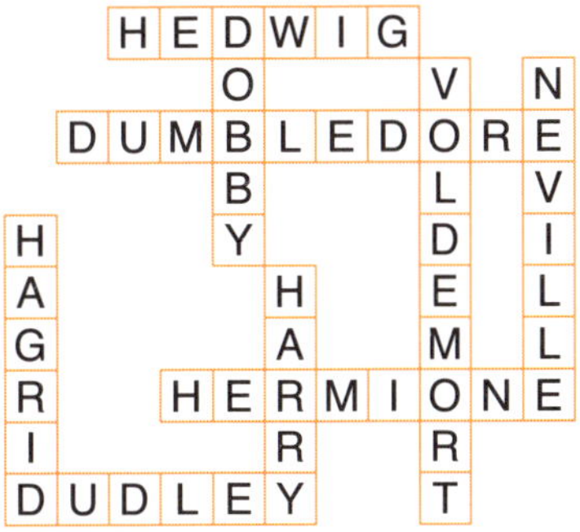

Drop Letters (page 12)

bugs; busy; bush; cubs; snub; stub

Letter Gridlock (page 13)

			C			
		P	E	R		
	B	A	R	E	S	
M	A	R	T	I	A	N
	G	I	A	N	T	
		S	I	S		
			N			

Come Together (page 14)

VENEZUELA

NICARAGUA

SINGAPORE

Theme Park (page 15)

				G	H	O	S	T	S	
				M	A	S	K			
		G	O	B	L	I	N	S		
					L					
				C	O	S	T	U	M	E
					W					
Z	O	M	B	I	E	S				
		M	A	K	E	U	P			
			C	A	N	D	Y			

Crunched Letters (page 16)

comet; women; homes

Crossed Out (page 17)

					S
					P
					R
					I
A	U	T	U	M	N
					G

Shuffle Board (page 17)

S	Q	U	A	D
	U			A
M	I	S	E	R
	E			T
I	T	E	M	S

Word Swatter (page 18)

Answers may vary.

SPOON NOTES

TOONS ASPEN

SNOOT SPENT

STOOP STONE

Fitting Tiles (page 19)

L	A	B	E	L
A	N	I	M	E
S	T	A	I	N
T	E	S	T	S

Drop Letters (page 20)

stir; trip; dirt; riot; grit; trim

Repeat Repeat (page 21)

POWERFUL

TOWEL

MACHINE

SPACING

Answers

Word Stickers (page 22)

BLACK NEAR

WHITE FAR

One Up (page 23)

SOUVENIRS

VERSIONS

SENIORS

SENSOR

SNORE

NOSE

SON

Alphabet Express (page 24)

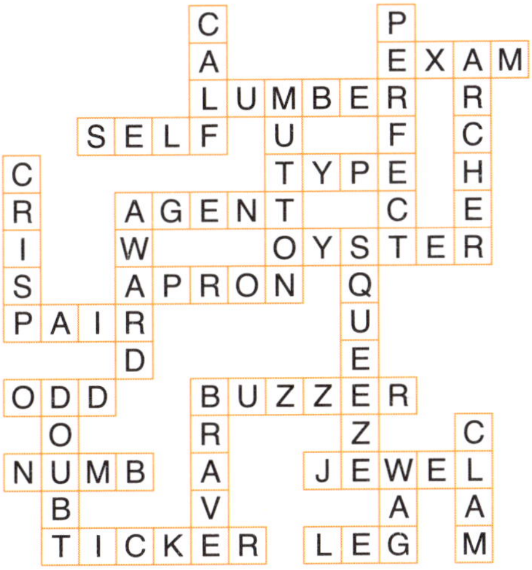

Letter Gridlock (page 25)

Jumbled Up (page 25)

Tile Tie-Ins (page 26)

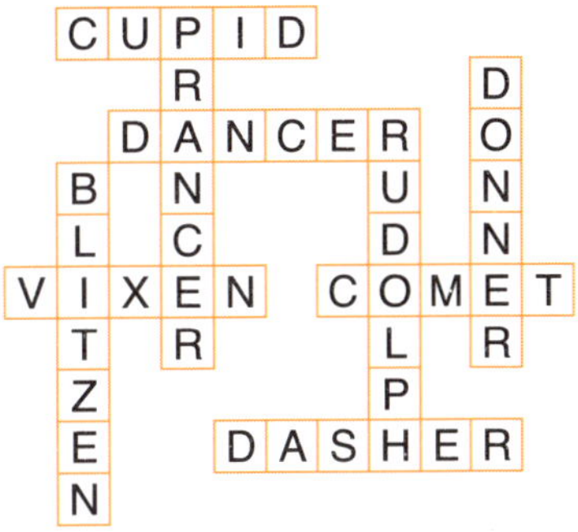

Piles o' Tiles (page 27)

Add-a-Letter (page 28)

DRIVE

IRON

CHIP

BIRDIE

EAGLE

TRAP

SLICE

Plus One (page 29)

Answers may vary.

LAMP	ACID
PALE	AIDE
FLAP	PAID

Word Swatter (page 30)

Answers may vary.

PAST

PATS

PUTS

TAPS

SPAT

Shuffle Board (page 31)

Answers may vary.

	P	A	L	M
	A			O
S	N	O	O	P
P		P		E
A		T		S

Reword Rewind (page 31)

rats/star

Crunched Letters (page 32)

blame; clamp; llama

Come Together (page 33)

ASPARAGUS

SPAGHETTI

CASSEROLE

Fitting Tiles (page 34)

M	A	J	O	R
U	S	A	G	E
L	I	B	R	A
E	A	S	E	L

Word Stickers (page 35)

FLOWER	STARE
FLOUR	STAIR

Theme Park (page 36)

SHARK

JELLYFISH

CLAM

OCTOPUS

SWORDFISH

GROUPER

STINGRAY

TUNA

SQUID

R

WHALE

PORPOISE

Shuffle Board (page 37)

A	S	P	S	
	P		T	
T	O	W	E	R
	R		A	
A	T	O	M	S

Crossed Out (page 37)

	D				
	A				
B	R	I	G	H	T
	K				

Alphabet Express (page 38)

G		T				Y	E	L	L	O	W
A	R	O	U	N	D			I		B	
R		T						Z		J	
B		A				S	H	A	V	E	R
A	X	L	E			M		R		C	
G			Q			O		D		T	
E			U			K					
		R	I	F	L	E					
			P								

Piles o' Tiles (page 39)

S	E	A	T	B	E	L	T
		I					
		S					
M		L				C	
O	V	E	R	H	E	A	D
V						R	
I						R	
E			T	R	A	Y	
						O	
C	A	P	T	A	I	N	

Drop Letters (page 40)

risk; kids; sick; skip; inks; silk

Chain Words (page 41)

Z	I	P	P	E	R	S	O	N

Reword Rewind (page 41)

crate/trace

Letter Gridlock (page 42)

			D			
		C	A	N		
	T	H	I	E	F	
Q	U	A	R	R	E	L
	G	L	I	D	E	
		K	E	Y		
			S			

Repeat Repeat (page 43)

STAPLER
HOSTILE

MARGARINE
SAGGING

One Up (page 44)

PARTICLES
REPLICAS
ECLAIRS
SERIAL
LIARS
AIRS
SIR

Tile Tie-Ins (page 45)

KRUSTY
MAGGIE
NELSON
MARGE
BART
RALPH
SKINNER
FLANDERS
LISA
MILHOUSE
HOMER

Crossed Out (page 46)

SOAKED
DRY

Word Swatter (page 46)

Answers may vary.

SPARED DRAPES
PADRES SPREAD

Add-a-Letter (page 47)

ROSE
IRIS
DAISY
LILAC
PEONY
ASTER
ORCHID

Drop Letters (page 48)

knew; news; when;
wane; anew; sewn

Piles o' Tiles (page 49)

M&MS
HOTTAMALES
SKITTLES
REESES
SOURPATCH
NERDS

Plus One (page 50)

Answers may vary.

SIFT PAWN
SITE PLAN
SKIT PANT

Letter Gridlock (page 51)

J
WES
IRATE
IRELAND
KNOTS
SUE
S

Come Together (page 52)

ALBATROSS
SAPSUCKER
CHICKADEE

Reword Rewind (page 53)

read/Dear

Chain Words (page 53)

SOCCEREAL

Word Stickers (page 54)

TIME — THYME

BAND — BANNED

Theme Park (page 55)

WINTERCLOTHES (down)

WOOLSOCKS
MITTENS
COAT
JACKET
EARMUFFS
SCARF
LONGUNDERWEAR
BOOTS
HAT
SWEATER
GLOVES

Crunched Letters (page 56)

decal; pecan; recap

Fitting Tiles (page 57)

N	E	I	G	H
A	U	D	I	O
P	R	O	V	E
S	O	L	E	S

One Up (page 58)

TANGERINE
ENTERING
INTEGER
ENTIRE
RETIE
TIER
TIE

Shuffle Board (page 59)

	B	E	A	T
		R		R
B	L	A	D	E
A				A
G	A	P	E	D

Word Swatter (page 60)

Answers may vary.

HUNT	SENT
NEST	NUTS
HENS	HUTS
NETS	STUN
SHUN	TUNE

Jumbled Up (page 60)

FREEZE

Repeat Repeat (page 61)

PENCILS
RECIPES

POPCORN
OFFSPRING

Add-a-Letter (page 62)

PINK
GOLD
GREEN
WHITE
BROWN
GRAY

Letter Gridlock (page 63)

			M			
		C	A	P		
	T	H	R	O	W	
F	A	I	R	I	E	S
	P	R	I	N	T	
		P	E	T		
			D			

Crossed Out (page 64)

			T	
			I	
			R	
H	Y	P	E	R
			D	

Tile Tie-Ins (page 65)

		A							
F		L	I	B	E	R	T	Y	
L		L							
A	M	E	R	I	C	A			J
G		G					S		U
		I		S	T	A	T	E	S
		A					A		T
		N	A	T	I	O	N		I
		C					D		C
P	L	E	D	G	E		S		E

Piles o' Tiles (page 66)

								M	
		G			B			E	
	S	A	T	E	L	L	I	T	E
		L			A			E	
S	T	A	R		C			O	
		X			K			R	
		Y			H				
				C	O	M	E	T	
					L				
					E				

Drop Letters (page 67)

past; path; spat; pita; atop; pant

Fitting Tiles (page 68)

H	A	T	C	H
A	L	O	H	A
S	T	E	A	M
H	O	S	T	S

One Up (page 69)

SKETCHING
KITCHENS
THICKEN
ETHNIC
NICHE
NICE
ICE

Word Stickers (page 70)

ABOVE EMPTY
BELOW FULL

Alphabet Express (page 71)

B	A	N	J	O						B				
R			U		H	O	R	I	Z	O	N	S		
E			D		A					X		Q		
E			G	A	V	E	L			E		U		
Z	O	N	E		E			P	E	R	H	A	P	S
E					N			A				W		A
								N				K		F
								I						E
								C	O	M	M	E	N	T
														Y

Shuffle Board (page 72)

		T		
F	E	A	R	S
E		K		H
T		E		U
A	S	S	E	T

Plus One (page 73)

Answers may vary.

GENE DASH
GLEE HEAD
GEEK HARD

Add-a-Letter (page 74)

BEANS
PEAS
SPINACH
BEETS
CORN
TURNIPS
ONIONS

Come Together (page 75)

ROCHESTER
MILWAUKEE
CLEVELAND

Crunched Letters (page 76)

canoe; canon; manor

Reword Rewind (page 76)

shop/hops

Theme Park (page 77)

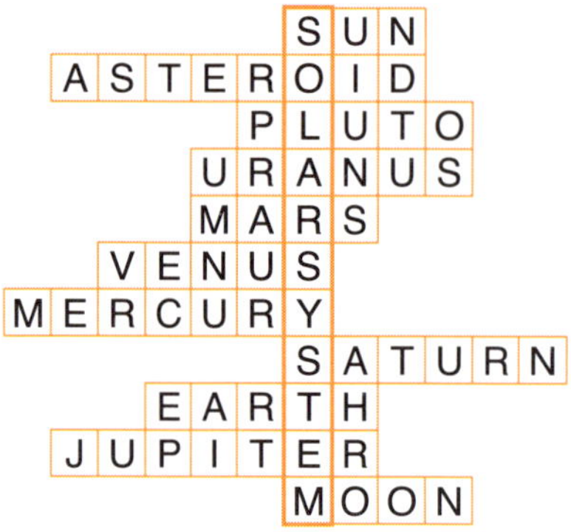

Tile Tie-Ins (page 78)

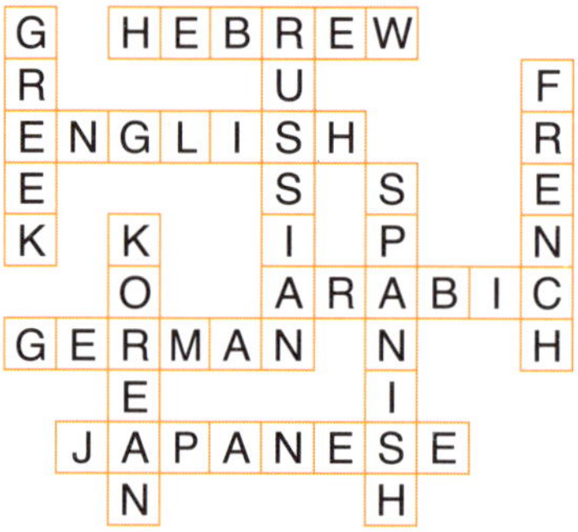

Letter Gridlock (page 79)

One Up (page 80)

THREATENS

THEATERS

SHATTER

HEARTS

EARTH

HEAT

HAT

Repeat Repeat (page 81)

BICYCLE

TICKLE

POWDERS

SPORTS

Tile Tie-Ins (page 82)

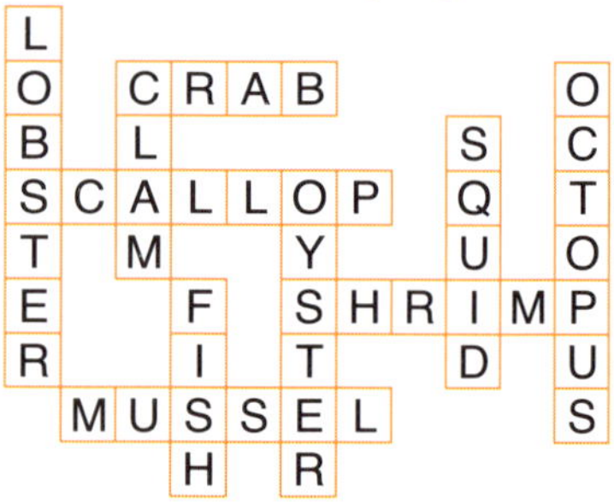

Crossed Out (page 83)

Chain Words (page 83)

PHONEVER

Come Together (page 84)

SPIDERMAN

DAREDEVIL

WOLVERINE

Plus One (page 85)

Answers may vary.

TRAP — TROT

TAPE — TOUT

TAPS — TOTE

Word Swatter (page 86)

Answers may vary.

OWES — WOES

AWES — COWS

ACES — CASE

Reword Rewind (page 86)

lemon/melon

Letter Gridlock (page 87)

Piles o' Tiles (page 88)

Alphabet Express (page 89)

Fitting Tiles (page 90)

F	A	I	R	Y
I	N	D	I	A
S	T	O	C	K
T	I	L	E	S

Answers

Add-a-Letter (page 91)

SCREAM
CREAK
GROAN
CRASH
BANG
SCRATCH
WHISPER

Theme Park (page 92)

CASE
TEXTING
LOL
CALL
PARENTS
HOME
RINGTONE
FRIENDS
EMERGENCY

(Down: CELLPHONE)

Drop Letters (page 93)

each; chew; echo;
ache; chef; etch

Shuffle Board (page 94)

P	E	A	L	■
E	■	I	■	P
T	O	R	S	O
A	■	■	■	S
L	E	A	S	T

Reword Rewind (page 94)

pans/naps/span

Crunched Letters (page 95)

fever; levee; seven

Chain Words (page 95)

MUFFINISH

Come Together (page 96)

NEWMEXICO
TENNESSEE
WISCONSIN

Piles o' Tiles (page 97)

Down: GREEN, ORANGE, VIOLET
Across: YELLOW, INDIGO, BLUE, RED

Repeat Repeat (page 98)

RESTAURANT
PETUNIA

GARLIC
GIRLIE

One Up (page 99)

RETALIATE

LITERATE

RETITLE

LITTER

LITER

TILE

LIE

Plus One (page 103)

Answers may vary.

STUB MOAN

BOUT MAIN

BUNT MANY

Alphabet Express (page 100)

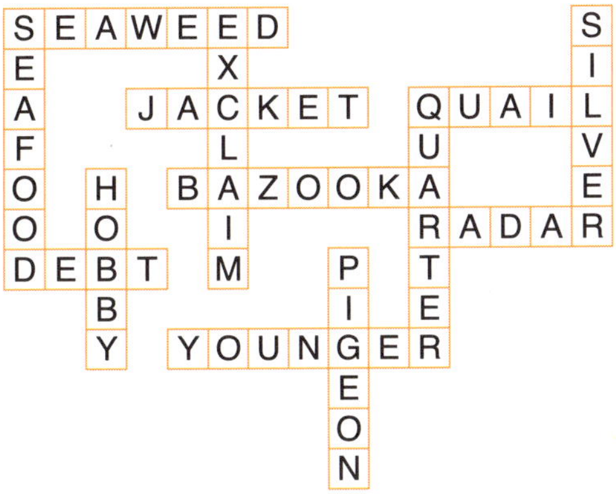

Tile Tie-Ins (page 104)

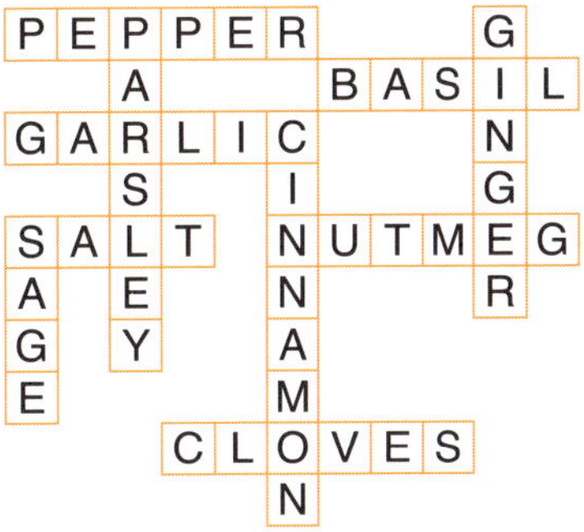

Word Stickers (page 101)

NOODLES CLOCK

PASTA TIMER

Piles o' Tiles (page 105)

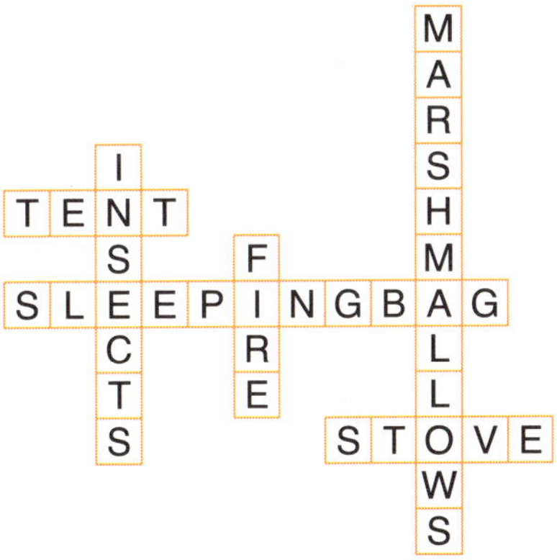

Letter Gridlock (page 102)

Add-a-Letter (page 106)

STAR
COMET
NOVA
WORLD
PLANET
ASTEROID

Crossed Out (page 107)

S			
K			
I			
L	U	C	K
L			

Word Swatter (page 108)

Answers may vary.

RACED	ACRES
RACES	CARDS
CARED	DARES
CARES	CEDAR
SCARE	READS

Drop Letters (page 109)

also; logs; slow; sold; soul; owls

Shuffle Board (page 110)

		W		S
	L	O	O	P
A		R		A
D	E	T	E	R
D		H		E

Jumbled Up (page 110)

JUDGE

Repeat Repeat (page 111)

WRINKLE
RANKED

BEACHBALL
CHALK

Crunched Letters (page 112)

eager; pager; wages

Jumbled Up (page 112)

THINK

Theme Park (page 113)

		T	A	B	L	E				
C	L	O	S	E	T					
				D	R	E	S	S	E	R
		M	I	R	R	O	R			
		C	L	O	C	K				
			P	O	S	T	E	R	S	
		L	A	M	P					

Fitting Tiles (page 114)

I	M	A	G	E
N	A	V	E	L
C	L	I	N	K
H	I	D	E	S

Tile Tie-Ins (page 115)

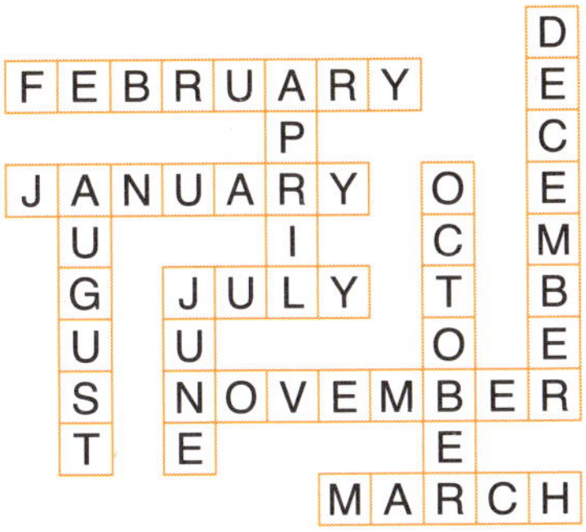

Reword Rewind (page 116)

free/reef

Crossed Out (page 117)

Chain Words (page 117)

DOZENJOY

Alphabet Express (page 118)

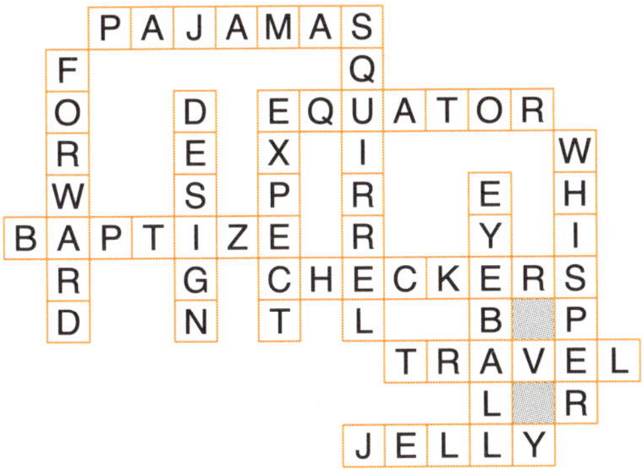

One Up (page 119)

CELEBRATE
BRACELET
TREACLE
CEREAL
CLEAR
LACE
ACE

Plus One (page 120)

Answers may vary.

HEMP	LOAD
HELM	LADY
THEM	GLAD

Drop Letters (page 121)

gulf; plug; ugly; glue; lung; gulp

Come Together (page 122)

LOUISIANA
MINNESOTA
NEWJERSEY

Piles o' Tiles (page 123)

	F								
	U				C				
I	N	V	I	T	A	T	I	O	N
			C		K				
	P	R	E	S	E	N	T	S	
			C						
		F	R	I	E	N	D	S	
			E						
			A						
			M						

Word Stickers (page 124)

B	E	A	S	T

S	P	A	R	E

M	O	N	S	T	E	R

E	X	T	R	A

Tile Tie-Ins (page 125)

M	O	S	C	O	W		C			T
A					A		A			O
D			B	E	R	L	I	N		K
R	O	M	E		S		R			Y
I			I		A		O	S	L	O
D			J		W				I	
			I						S	
V	I	E	N	N	A				B	
			G						O	
				D	U	B	L	I	N	

Add-a-Letter (page 126)

D	R	E	S	S		
S	K	I	R	T		
P	A	N	T	S		
S	C	A	R	F		
S	W	E	A	T	E	R
J	E	A	N	S		
S	H	A	W	L		

Theme Park (page 127)

			B	U	R	P		
	D	I	A	P	E	R		
			B	O	T	T	L	E
	S	P	I	T	U	P		
C	R	I	E	S				
N	U	R	S	E				

Fitting Tiles (page 128)

D	I	T	C	H
A	D	I	E	U
T	E	E	N	S
E	A	R	T	H

Crunched Letters (page 129)

cough; gouge; tough

Jumbled Up (page 129)

Letter Gridlock (page 130)

			G			
		W	O	E		
	H	E	A	L	S	
M	A	I	L	B	O	X
	T	R	I	O	S	
		D	E	W		
			S			

Crossed Out (page 131)

			F	
			R	
D	A	T	E	D
			S	
			H	

Answers

Drop Letters (page 132)

wide; owed; weld;
drew; awed; dewy

Plus One (page 133)

Answers may vary.

ANTE WARN
AUNT WAND
WANT SWAN

Repeat Repeat (page 134)

PREMIERE
SPIDERS

ANIMALS
SNAILS

Reword Rewind (page 135)

taste/state

Chain Words (page 135)

GLOBALLET

One Up (page 136)

NIGHTMARE
EMIGRANT
GARMENT
MAGNET
AGENT
GATE
AGE

Come Together (page 137)

BARREDOWL
NIGHTHAWK
HOUSEWREN

Word Swatter (page 138)

Answers may vary.

TABLES STABLE
TABLET BATTLE
BEETLE LATEST

Alphabet Express (page 139)

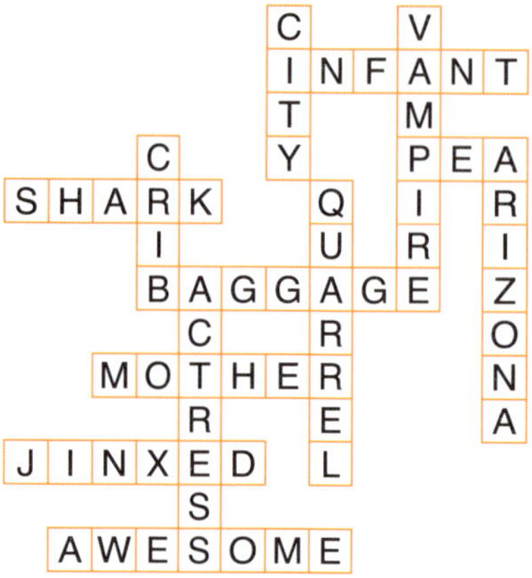

Theme Park (page 140)

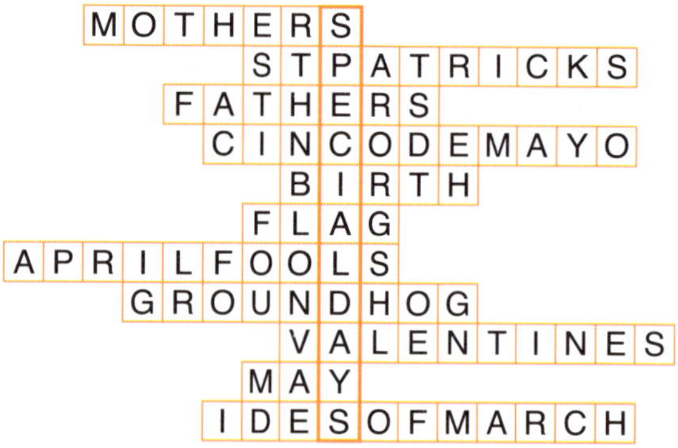

Fitting Tiles (page 141)

G	H	O	S	T
N	E	V	E	R
A	R	E	N	A
W	O	R	D	Y

Tile Tie-Ins (page 142)

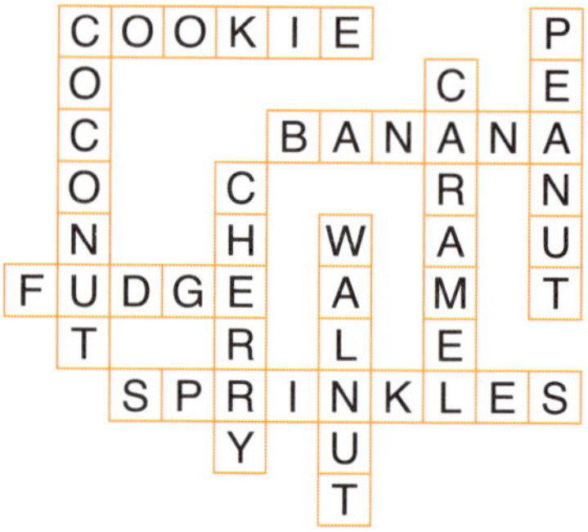

Crunched Letters (page 143)

cater; latex; water

Jumbled Up (page 143)

Piles o' Tiles (page 144)

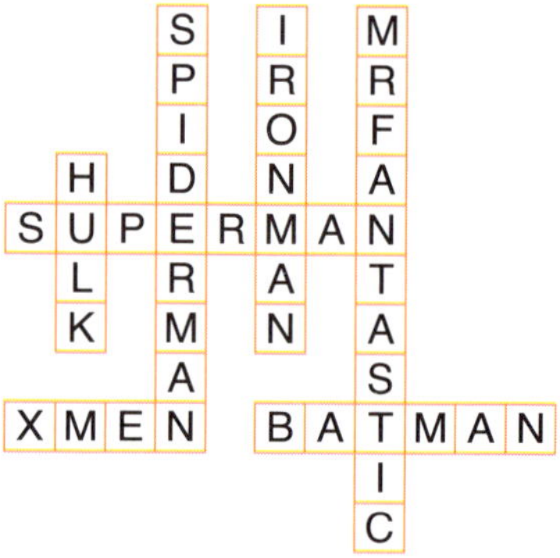

Shuffle Board (page 145)

U	S	E		T
	P			A
T	A	P	E	R
	C			P
P	E	A	R	S

Add-a-Letter (page 146)

BRICK

CREAM

EDAM

GOAT

FETA

CHEDDAR

GOUDA

Repeat Repeat (page 147)

SHERIFF
SHELF

MACARONI
CROWNS

Word Stickers (page 148)

BLEW

BLUE

CELLAR

SELLER

Letter Gridlock (page 149)

			C			
		P	O	P		
	G	O	R	E	S	
H	A	U	N	T	E	D
	S	T	R	A	W	
		S	O	L		
			W			

Come Together (page 150)

BALDEAGLE

BLACKBIRD

GOLDFINCH

Jumbled Up (page 151)

NUMBER

Repeat Repeat (page 152)

KITCHEN
THICKEN

FLORIDA
FORCED

One Up (page 153)

BUTTERFLY

FLUTTERY

UTTERLY

TURTLE

UTTER

TRUE

RUT

Word Swatter (page 154)

Answers may vary.

```
P O I N T
P I N T S
P I N T O
```

Theme Park (page 155)

```
      C A N A D A
    K O R E A
      U S A
C H I N A
    I T A L Y
      R U S S I A
M E X I C O
      E N G L A N D
  A U S T R A L I A
```

Tile Tie-Ins (page 156)

```
                    S
              C     Q
T R A P E Z O I D   U
  H   E       R     A
P O I N T     C     R
  M   T       L I N E
  B   A N G L E
  U   G
  S   O C T A G O N
      N
```

Fitting Tiles (page 157)

```
C A I R O
A R R O W
S T I L L
E S S E S
```

Chain Words (page 158)

```
E A R T H I N K
```

Crossed Out (page 158)

```
      S
      W
      E
      E
S A L T Y
```

Plus One (page 159)

Answers may vary.

```
A F A R     H U G S
F A I R     H U G E
F A R M     H U N G
```

Crunched Letters (page 160)

bones; honey; loner

Reword Rewind (page 161)

Bran/barn

Word Stickers (page 161)

```
Q U I E T     S L E E P Y
M U T E D     T I R E D
```

Add-a-Letter (page 162)

```
A U T O
L I M O
B O A T
S E D A N
S H I P
T R A I N
```

Come Together (page 163)

P	A	R	T	R	I	D	G	E

S	A	N	D	P	I	P	E	R

B	L	A	C	K	T	E	R	N

Alphabet Express (page 164)

								B	L	A	N	K	E	T
	C							E		D				O
	A				R			H		M				W
F	R	E	E	Z	E		T	A	X	I				E
	E				F			V		R	O	G	E	R
	F		S	Q	U	A	R	E		E				
J	U	M	P		S									
	L		R		E									
			A											
			Y											

Drop Letters (page 165)

inch; coin; icon; nice; chin; zinc

Letter Gridlock (page 166)

			T			
		R	O	W		
	J	E	E	R	S	
P	E	N	N	I	E	S
	T	E	A	S	E	
		W	I	T		
			L			

Shuffle Board (page 167)

S	L	E	E	P
P				E
A	R	M		A
I				C
N	O	R	T	H

Jumbled Up (page 168)

A	N	S	W	E	R

Crossed Out (page 168)

	F		
	R		
	E		
	E		
	Z		
M	E	L	T

Alphabet Express (page 169)

G						J	U	S	T	
R	A	I	N	S		A			H	
A				T		M	E	T	A	L
C	O	W	B	O	Y				N	
E				V					K	
				E	X	I	T		F	
							R		U	
					E	Q	U	A	L	
					C		M			
					H		P			
				D	O	Z	E	N		
							T			

Theme Park (page 170)

					V	I	O	L	I	N				
			H	O	R	N								
						S	A	X	O	P	H	O	N	E
			F	L	U	T	E							
					T	R	O	M	B	O	N	E		
					T	U	B	A						
			D	R	U	M								
			O	B	O	E								
	C	L	A	R	I	N	E	T						
T	R	U	M	P	E	T								
C	Y	M	B	A	L	S								